A Feeling for
ROCK

Sarah-Jane Dobner

'… that first thrilling glimpse of a crag through mist or rain or sunshine: rock waiting, like a lover, to be loved.'

Gwen Moffat, 2018

'It is argued that rock climbing may be fruitfully understood as a network of interrelations between humans, within humans, between humans and nonhuman natures (the latter including rocks, cliffs, vegetation, water, and animals), and between humans and other nonhumans (e.g., technologies, objects, and texts). Through the rude intermingling of these various entities, cliffs become climbs and humans become climbers; each becomes impurely different and different spaces are born.'

Penelope Rossiter, 2007

A Feeling for Rock

CONTENTS

CONTENTS

DEVOTION

Devotion:
A Sensational Passion

Rock climbing has shaped my body, my bookshelves, my boyfriends, my community, my employment, my home, my holidays, the clothes I wear, the vehicle I drive, how I spend my money and what happens when I die. I am a product of the rock. The dynamic is visceral, spiritual, intellectual and emotional – no area of me untouched by this curious hobby.

My aim in writing this is to communicate how it *feels* to belay at the top of a cliff, or tackle a crux, or leaf through a guidebook. To illustrate the heartfelt connection and physical experience. Suggest a few passionate, sensual destinations which it might be fun to explore or revisit. Plus cartoons, interviews, ethical ideas and technical tips.

Rock Is the Earth's Truth

You can't bullshit on a trad lead. There can be any amount of talk beforehand but once the leader is tracing a line over the curving sheet of rock above, you get to see how they are. Not just as a climber but as a person. Are they bold or timid, jerky or balletic, logical or illogical, careful or reckless, loud and attention-seeking or silent and gripped? You see how they are this particular day, in this moment, out in the sun-dappled afternoon.

I love this rawness. It's the key that takes climbing from a bit of exercise into the existential sphere. We are stripped down and questions are asked.

Who are we? Why are we here? Now religion is fallible and meditation so deathly dull, where do we look for guidance? The numbing cushion of comforts and convenience smothers us all; pleasantries cloud our conversations. What is the reality of life on this planet? That we can die at any second. That we breathe air. That it is beautiful.

Rock is the earth's truth. It is the molten heart come to light, the deepest layers scoured out. Every fragment of rock has been made in torment: crushed, boiled, compressed. And millennia later it is revealed in agony:

squeezed through the earth's crust, cut through by ice, whipped by winds. What else in the landscape has suffered as much? Trees grow gently. The grass photosynthesises at its own pace. Water in seas and glaciers and lakes and skies changes form but slips through these various metamorphoses without much strife and all stages are fully reversible. But rock? Rock is different. Every outcrop is a monument to pain, each gorge a terrific scar.

And the rock will stick its neck out, telling that truth. The lone pinnacles of the desert towers of Utah, the low black granite tors of Dartmoor, the sliced-open anatomy of Yosemite. Everything is laid bare.

I find a good deal of comfort in rock. It has suffered this much and still stands tall. It will shelter me like an older brother should and for a time my small anxieties are put into perspective, put aside. Climbing a rock face is to connect, for a time, with the cutting edge of life, with the bones of the world. No padding. No fluff.

In everyday life, where else do we see people with so little guard? Where they are crying, yelling, soiling their pants in fear? Maybe you'd see these things in a warzone. Or a funeral. Occasionally when someone's very, very drunk. When do you see people trying this hard? Grunting and hyperventilating, disco-legged and super-pumped, with no regard to prettiness, still keeping going, still trying, giving it their all? It's an honour to share these levels of revelation with another human being. We are human beings. We are terrified. We love. The tiling of your bathroom is of no interest to me. I don't care if my clothes aren't stylish. No, I don't recognise your brand of car.

Let us get down to the truth. We could die at any second. We breathe air. It is beautiful.

Astonishment:
At Great Heights

It took me a long time to start rock climbing as I was scared of heights.

One of my friends took up the sport, and was always persuading me to try. But I declined. For ten years I occasionally accompanied her on trips, where I would go hiking while she climbed. One weekend in Pembroke sticks in my mind. Remember watching her crew roped up and faffing at a minor crag and I took my map and went striding for miles and miles, all the way along the Range, ducking into every bay, stopping to look at seals and seabirds and when I got back they were still on the same cliff and I thought that was stupid and didn't envy them one bit.

As is the way of things, I began dating one of her acquaintances. By this time I was in my late twenties, with a child. The Firestarter took me to the Peak District and led up a route whilst I fumbled the safety equipment ineffectually. My first climb was seconding that low lump of grit. It was damp and dreadful. I didn't trust the ropes and was terrified by the drop. Yet I'm eternally grateful for that inauspicious introduction, as whilst girlfriending the

Firestarter only lasted eighteen months, I was left with a more enduring relationship. For all intents and purposes, I married the rock.

It's like we settled down together to do the crossword. The mental challenge of rockovers, slabs and laybacks kept me engaged. The touch and movement were altogether more physical. A romance. I became obsessed with my queer love-interest. Never a jealous arrangement – granite, limestone, sandstone, dolerite, Welsh mountain rock – I've played with them all. On winter evenings, drift around the bouldering gym, eyeing up the butch overhangs and smiling just a little at the cute, dinky crimps.

We have spent two happy decades together. Most of the time, the tactile glory and code-cracking are so all-consuming, I lack the surplus energy to be frightened of heights. Just occasionally – a free-hanging abseil onto a wave-cut platform with a big sea running, or unpeeling my fingers from the lower-off when I haven't climbed indoors for a while – I'll be flooded with the ancient fear. Deep inside.

So it's still there.

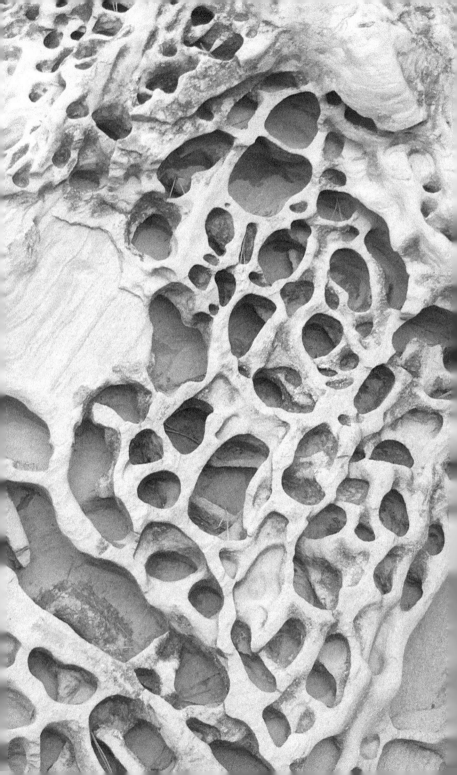

Relief:

Touch

Slab

Lay your cheek
On the slab
That giant's chest
And count the breaths

Place your open
Palm flat
On the rock face
And feel for a pulse

Skin

Gentle, exploratory sweeps
Whorls at the tips tickling and testing
Dipping and dunking, fumbling and fingering
Gripping. Over-clinging. Stroking. Smoothing

Rock that is crozzly, knobbly, crystalline, dusty
Rasping, glass-smooth, wafer-layered, crumbling
And from time to time so soft and warm
It feels like skin

Braille

A braille of comprehension
Fingers assessing the meaning
Of fine-grain friction
Subtle edges and crystals

Cross-referencing the incut
At the back of the crack
Understanding the import
Of out-of-sight overlaps

A glossary of touch. Deciphering
Limestone hieroglyphics
Or the art-house
Literature of grit

Bruises

Don't clock the bruises
Find them later
Doing a double-take
In the bluish light of the tent

Cuticles shredded and bleeding
Only obvious
When tips slicken with blood
And compromise your grip

Grazes on shoulders
Scabbed knees
A brutal passion this
So enthralled you didn't notice

Venus

Full body contact
This embrace. Throw
My arms around the climb

At the base of El Capitan
Hug the tip of the nose
And smooth the face

At Stanage, lie
Against the bare skin, breathe
Its smell of hay and tummy buttons

Stroke the granite at Bonehill
On Dartmoor. Seek out
Dimples and pimples

With the familiarity
Of birds which clean the backs
Of rhinoceroses

Or Pentire. Be bold enough
To touch the world's
Nakedness

As the cliff
Rises out of the unfurling waters
Like Venus

Confusion:

Better than Sex?

Fifteen years ago, lying in bed on a Saturday morning, Mad Dog, flushed with hanky-panky, declaimed, 'There's nothing better than this!' I recollect my instant swing from pleasure to alarm. Nothing better! There was Central Groove on the Dewerstone! And we had better get cracking if we wanted a decent day! From that moment, and at odd times since, I've posed myself the question, *If I had to choose between climbing and sex, which one would it be?*

Today, for example, I am once again contemplating this dilemma. I'm in a foul mood. My pencilled-in climbing day didn't happen as it is drizzling miserably and blowing a gale. Practised the guitar but played all the wrong notes; started painting some tulips but they only made me cross. I roamed about the house like a lost wildebeest. Then, early afternoon, Bass String came in and strode defiantly across the carpet in his football boots, shin-pads and shorts, showcasing an entertaining length of thigh. He made himself strong, black coffee on the stove-top. I stampeded the kitchen but he was having none of it and headed straight back out, caffeine-boosted for the match.

Climbing. Sex. They hit the same buttons in many

ways. The dance of them, the physicality, the risk-taking, the exploration of the unknown. Whilst other activities are time-fillers, sex and climbing are the real thing. Necessary. Addictive. And the chemicals! Those stupendous drugs we manufacture, endorphins and adrenaline cooked up in the same crucible of desire. But which to choose? I tramp up and down the stairs, a disgruntled gnu, weighing up the odds.

Climbing takes up a lot of time and that's an advantage. When picking an activity for life it seems wise to select the one which starts early morning and ends way after dinner; the diversion which lasts day after day on a week-long holiday. However tantric one's approach in bed surely things would peter out after the first eight-hour stint? Assuming you're not John and Yoko. Climbing wins.

Climbing is more reliable. Boyfriends come and go. Sex waxes and wanes. Whatever the vicissitudes of a relationship, the rock is always there. Rock will never be absent, forget to turn up or have a headache. Climbing comes out on top.

On the other hand, sex isn't as dangerous. Climbing is inherently unsafe so death, paralysis, serious injury are all possible, whatever precautions you take. By contrast, given a stable partner and mutual STD tests we are insulated from syphilis and AIDS. Clearly, a predilection for simulated strangulation or extreme S&M might tip the balance the other way but, even so, surely soloing El Capitan is more hazardous? King Of Kings wasn't convinced and bleakly commented, 'I could have my willie chopped off while I slept! Or wake up being stabbed in the heart and it's all over.' But on the basis I know plenty of people who've broken their ankles climbing and none who've had their willies chopped off, I'll stick with sex.

And how good's the glow? Both pretty damn good. The warm satisfaction of an everyday coupling or an unspectacular day trip is possibly equally nice. But recollection of a really good day out climbing can, years later, trigger a body-memory of wonder: the brutal joy of topping out at the Black Canyon; the vivid thrill of onsighting Break On Through at Sharpnose. Recalling my more splendid sexual encounters will summon a happy rush from tip to toe. However, being tinged with absurdity – the way sex is – in all honesty I'd have to throw my chips in with climbing.

Is there any financial weighting? Climbing I've always thought of as an inexpensive hobby; once you've bought the kit you can have numerous amazing epics for the price of the diesel. Other adventure sports – paragliding, diving, skiing – are much more costly. Sex is free though. Sex wins hands down.

Which to choose? After all these years I'm still not sure. I figured I might plump for climbing if push came to shove. But what if I got injured and couldn't climb any more, and was left with neither? What if the passion faded, and I eloped with mountain biking? What if Bass String wore football shorts all the time? Sex? Climbing? Climbing? Sex? Happily, of course, I don't have to choose. Thank goodness! It's like waking from a dream where you've driven your van off a cliff and then you remember, it's just a dream! *The van's still parked outside!* I don't have to choose! Climbing *and* sex. I'm allowed both.

Just not today. Not now it's dark and the drizzle has turned to rain. Not now that Bass String's off playing football then working nights. Climbing. Sex. One of them soon please. Either will do.

Appreciation:
All the Natural Formations

Clefts, chasms, crevices, rifts, ravines, runnels, splitters, slits, slots, zawns, pockets, holes, chimneys, fissures, gashes, grooves, cracks.

Towers, tors, chickenheads, outcrops, nobbles, needles, projections, pinnacles, pillars, columns, spires, spikes.

Slabs, walls, overlaps, roofs, domes, conglomerate.

Lust:

Rock Erotica

Excerpt from a proposal to an academic publication for inclusion in their mountaineering special edition (rejected)

Western culture maintains a hierarchy which puts humans above cats above pot plants above rocks. So when sea cliffs cradle me, I know I am stepping into zones of perversity. When touch needs are met by the crystal play of granite, this transgresses decency. The erotic is entangled with everything else (Barad 2007). I feel it. But this is loose, XS territory.

> My love of the rock is not innocent
> Driving to the crag
> The thrill
> In the pit of my stomach…

That frisson.

A passion over decades, promiscuous with kinks, bouldering at Fontainebleau, multi-pitch trad on Welsh mountains, I have thrown myself at the foot of many a crag seeking that brutal, airy relief.

> …Shameless. Sinking
> Fists into cracks
> Fingering lips
> Will it…hold…hurt…fit?…

Skinning my knee on the overhang, gritty flesh, bloody outcrop, dirty games. Rossiter talks of the 'rude intermingling' of rock and climbers (2007: 293).

> …Desire draws me up and up
> If I fall
> The rock can have me
> Any which way it likes…

Rock climbing as a place of intimacy regarding touch, companionship and sexual charge. How welcome are these sentiments in mountain culture?

Top Tips for Transitions

Plastic to Rock (Bouldering)

1. Love the rock. It is your ally, not your adversary. It will help you and take care of you and guide you. Before starting to climb, perhaps take a moment to sit with the boulders. Get to know each other. It's rude to touch without being introduced.

2. Stand on your feet. Outdoor climbs are often much slabbier than indoor problems. Walk up. Feel the rock through your snug rubber boots.

3. Go into 3D mode. Everything is a hold – the entire surface of the blank groove, the dimpled wall, the projection behind you. To meet this, your whole body becomes a tool (your back, seat, forearms, elbows), not just hands and toes.

4. Mind your ankles. It's easy to miss a boulder mat and landings can be rocky. Get into the habit of climbing up and down with care. Check the top-outs before committing.

5. Climb from the inside. Feel how your body wants to move. Trust your flesh, and its connection with the

rock. This isn't about showing off to anyone else or 'ticking'/'conquering' a particular problem.

6. Be willing to learn. You are the pupil, rock is the teacher. Concentrate in class, whatever limestone, sandstone or granite is the lesson. Accept your bashed cuticles, bloodied knees and bruised ego. Outdoors is old school so be respectful: try hard, take the punishment and don't answer back!

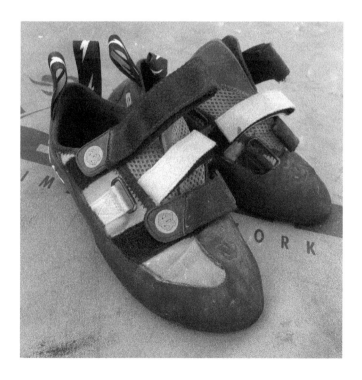

Indoor Routes to Outdoor Sport Climbing

1. Get into the habit of researching access and suitability. Check weather (rainfall, wind speed and direction), tide times, bird bans, firing notices, owner restrictions, recent rockfall, etc. The BMC RAD app is a good place to start.

2. Take the easiest line. Move around. Only rarely will the route follow bolts like a piece of string. What does the rock want you to do? Where does it want you to go? Your movements aren't dictated by human setters with a plan in their head. You're dealing with a cosmic setter out there. Tune in. A good rule of thumb is to choose the pathway with the best footholds (don't worry so much about the hands).

3. Learn new techniques. Some movements which are used occasionally indoors become absolute mainstays outside. So palming down, for instance, really comes into its own on real rock. Become acquainted with jamming, mantleshelving, back-and-footing and other comedy horrorshows. Ask people to help you.

4. Be quiet. Not making a racket is part of the etiquette. Learn the climbing calls. Aside from these, do not shout loudly up and down the length of the cliff. Especially do not swear, power scream or go on about how hard you climb indoors. Such noisiness distracts everyone else from listening to the crag.

5. Wear a helmet. It would be my suggestion. Rocks break. Quickdraws get dropped by mistake. It won't guarantee your safety, but it might help.

6. Pace yourself. An indoor route might take five to ten minutes, while leading an outdoor sport route may take half an hour or more. Don't rush, don't panic, don't apologise. Take the time the route demands. Keep going steadily upwards.

Sport to Traditional Climbing

1. Be honest with yourself. Are you fierce today? Reckless? Emotionally wobbly? Take all this into account, because what is inside tends to manifest on the rock. Trad is less about your fingers and more about your soul.

2. Move from rest to rest. Look up and clock where your next rest will be and move to that. If you get blocked, step down a few feet and replan. Why take or hang when you can just bridge out and stand in balance? Though this feels unfashionable, it will build awareness and strategy and stamina. Try it.

3. Foster partnerships with people you trust. With trad you will commonly end up out of sight and out of hearing. You need to be very clear what the rope movements are likely to mean and how to respond. Communicate with each other before you set off.

4. Really get to know the rock and, by extension, the gear (wires, cams, slings, etc). If, in sport, you can climb on top of the rock, clipping bolt to bolt, with trad you must go deeper. Look in the slots. Feel in the cracks. And always the question is – will the rock protect you? How well? Do you rate that cam a 1/5 or a 4/5? Will it hold you if you fall? Develop your judgment. Open your heart to trust. Trad, for me, is where the relationship with the cliff shifts from pleasantries to

intimate exchanges about things that matter.

5. Be prepared to make it an apprenticeship. Transitioning from hard sport to tick a few select E6s has always left me cold. Opposing wires, chimneys, loose top-outs, abseil access, multi-pitch route-finding, double ropes tracing the cliff parallel as tramlines – how to become competent with all of this? Many years on many different crags having many epics. Try and keep the epics reasonably safe.

6. Hide your sandwiches. Otherwise they will surely be eaten by seagulls/mice/squirrels/cows/flies/dogs.

Encouragement:
Day One

I recently got chatting to Clara, Ebony and Alice at my local bouldering gym. They were new to climbing. How did they feel about it?

Clara: I'm Clara, and I've been rock climbing for a few months, I'd say. After I rock climbed a bit when I was younger.

Ebony: I'm Ebony. And this is my first day climbing. Yeah!

Alice: I'm Alice. And this is also my first day climbing. Yip!

Clara: Like, it's overcoming this – these little challenges, that you don't really get to experience in everyday life. When you think that you can't do it. And you're really stuck on a / on a bit and you feel like you wanna just come down – but / and you're holding on and you're trying to use all your strength to hold on and then you think – *Oh no! Maybe I can just go over there – or move slightly on this side* – and then you grab it – and that feeling of achievement that you get is so simple – but so satisfying.

And you really feel like you did that in your body.

And – I don't know – it's just / It's just an amazing feeling.

Alice: It's about learning to trust yourself and your abilities and the body that you have. And with that – feeling confident inside of your body, I think.

Clara: Hmmm. And your strength.

Alice: And also I feel like we don't really use our bodies for that much. Any more. And so – I don't know – we can become lazy so easily /

Clara: And we're all not that active, as people. But rock climbing you really use all your body at once /

Alice: Also it's just a very enjoyable sport.

Clara: And your brain.

Alice: Like it's such an overall good feeling in every muscle. Learning patience and to be patient with your body.

Ebony: And my idea of it was totally different to what it actually is.

Clara: Yeah, me too.

Ebony: I thought it was sort of about / there's this idea of *Oh look at me, I'm really strong!* – and everything – and *I have no fear!* – and *I'm going to get to the top and I'm going to do it really quick*. About being quick and fierce and strong.

          And it can be that.

          But it's actually more about how the / while you're doing it / not just – *Okay I'm here at the bottom and now I want to get to the top*. But the middle bit. Everything. Doing it really slow. Taking it in. Thinking about it. Where's your hand going to go? Where's your feet going to go?

And then the getting back down as well.

Like when you sit there and you watch other people do it, that are, like, really good and they do it as / it's like a meditation thing, you know. Like every day, they're always coming – and they're doing it really slow.

And really thinking about it /

Clara: And it was like – moving – your – leg /

Ebony: Their minds are really into it /

Clara: Moving your arm –

Ebony: And they're like breathing really slow. It's not about – like – you know.

I like it.

Clara: One thing I was saying is, like, any ability can do it. Which is so cool. Cos there's no / it's not really competitive. It's just competitive in yourself, of like, trying to achieve something that you couldn't do before. And yeah – we're all different abilities – and we can all do it.

Alice: And so just encouraging each other. Just like learning encouragement. And accepting encouragement. And also accepting achievement as well. In others and in yourself. Like –

Ebony: Trust is a big one isn't it. Like if you're not very good at it, like me – you'll be like *Try this, do that*, and then if you do it, and it works, you've, like, overcome something. You've learned to trust someone else's direction – which is nice.

When we went over that bit there – you know the bit that goes round and then down – I was nearly crying! I was so scared! But then we did it now.

So I'm really happy.

Clara: And then next time you'll know that you can do it. So you'll do it better.

Ebony: I probably wouldn't have done it unless you were both there though. I'd have probably gone back down.

Clara: But that's really good that you did it.

Ebony: Yeah, it's nice.

PRIDE

Pride:
Climb Like a Girl

There was a campaign called 'Like a Girl' launched in 2014. The video featured women and men and boys doing activities 'like a girl' where they were flopsy and pathetic and ineffective; this was contrasted with footage of actual girls who, when asked to do the same activities 'like a girl', ran and punched and threw balls in a powerful way. The video went viral.

Have you ever heard anyone (a guy?) shout out that someone is climbing like a girl, meaning that person isn't trying and is faffing around and being generally useless? It's a poor use of language. Words change the way we feel about ourselves. Let's make 'like a girl' a good thing. The way doing something 'like a man' is seen as a compliment. Hell, let's go the whole hog and make doing something 'like a woman' a damned fine accolade too.

Right then. Back to girls. And why it's amazing to climb like a girl. For if we're going to make generalisations on gender stereotypes, it's widely appreciated that women and girls often climb with great technique. Often better technique than guys. That's what 'climb like a girl' should mean. That you're showing great technique.

My friend Trevor Massiah has been teaching climbing for thirty years; he now runs the guiding-coaching-climbing holiday company Rock & Sun. He's made it his life's work to study how people climb. We're sitting at the foot of the crag sharing yesterday's prawn stir-fry from a tupperware box.

'Women and girls generally have better technique,' he says bluntly. 'The way to get good is to start off weak! And keen! Then you have to learn good technique from day one.'

As luck would have it, women are typically blessed with less upper body strength than men. And so we have to work out better technique. Better technique invariably means better footwork, pushing up with both legs, using efficient movement, rather than brute force.

But quite often these skills are unsung. Climbing magazines and popular culture can slip off into the celebration of fitness regimes, campus boarding, core work, summit-bagging, mountain-conquering, protein shakes, dynos and one finger pull-ups. These are all rather masculine glories.

'Have you noticed,' continues Trevor, 'how focused people are on training at the moment?'

'Yes, Trev, I have! The glamorisation of strength! The pornification of power! I'm all about resting and doing less,' I say smugly.

'But what about technique?'

'These days I mainly eat lunch,' I counter.

Look around. Look at the vocabulary and images that surround us. Take climbing films. There is often an implicit, unconscious weighting towards power over technique. So the camera may focus on the fingers and arms, upper body, muscles bulging, fingertips crushing, and only occasionally pull back so you can see a full body view of how the climber is really being propelled, usually by their excellent footwork. Similarly, guidebook descriptions might say, 'Move up the slab using a stiff pull'; shouldn't it be saying, 'Push up nicely on your feet'? This is a slab, remember. We tell beginners to focus on their feet but thereafter every subliminal message is that power and cranking hard is where it's at.

Clearly this is a reflection of underlying values. So a woman's skill on slabs, say, is unlikely to attract the same attention as a man's skill on a big overhang. Look at indoor walls for instance; in terms of transferable technique for outdoor climbing, the majority of the panels should be vertical or slabs. But indoor walls are overwhelmingly steep and overhanging. Partly that's because off-vertical walls give a clean, safer fall. I understand that. But is the steepness also geared towards what men enjoy? And what they do well? How many women get consulted and listened to when walls are designed?

Lately, Trevor has codified a sequence of movements, which puts the focus on footwork and not pulling with your arms. He's dubbed it 'The Secret'. It's a world away from power screams and foot-free lock-offs. It's quiet and steady and good technique. It's the way, in particular, that many girls and women already climb.

The climbing community is actually pretty good. It's a lot better than many sports in terms of gender representation and equality. It's not as advanced as tennis. But it's better than snooker. However, as in many other areas of life, the management committees of climbing bodies are dominated by men; the majority of climbing magazines are run by men. There are many reasons for this. But it's good to simply be aware that we are not seeing a true reflection of our sport.

And what would our media look like if it reflected men and women equally? If fifty per cent of writers, photographers, editors, owners and distributors were women? It's so unfamiliar I can barely imagine it. Perhaps there would be more articles on the spiritual aspects of multi-pitch sea cliffs. More artwork. More poetry on the feeling of moving on rock. More attention to the tiny strawberry plants where we flake out our ropes. More shared experience of a community of climbers. Who knows? We're still in a world where people shout 'You're climbing like a girl!' as an insult.

And why don't girls and women object when they feel

offended by a stray comment? Unfortunately, women are habituated to being shouted at in the street and trolled on the Internet. Why don't they press for more representation? Lack of representation is endemic, in business, finance, politics and the media; we're used to it. It seems normal. But it's not normal. And it's not inevitable.

I can get quite wound up at the entrenched inequality and small comments can set my mind spinning. Trevor is always a comfort; 'Things are getting better and better, SJ. Look at the changes in the last fifty years! There has never been a better time to be Black or to be a woman.' And he's right. I'm just impatient. I'm not going to live forever and progress isn't happening fast enough.

'Right then,' says Trev. 'This next route looks great.' We tidy the food away and get back to getting up sheer rock faces on our hands and feet. It's Trev's turn to lead. He touches the limestone gently and moves his toe-point to a small foothold, only a few inches up, level with his shin. 'Sometimes the clients watch me climb,' he says, turning to me, 'and they say to me *You climb like a girl.*'

He looks thoroughly chuffed.

Curiosity:
The Puzzle

Puzzles baited the line.

There I was, swimming along the mainstream, occupied with a toddler and a nascent profession, when climbing yanked me out of the river. Brain-work was the maggot, the worm! How to scale this barely textured wall? How to vault the overhang or ascend this jagged crack? I was repeatedly flummoxed. There appeared to be dozens of different ways to move. It called for shapes I had no idea my body could make. Which methods succeeded and which failed when faced with a glorious, unique, multi-faceted piece of stone? It blew my mind. I swallowed the grub and gobbled the hook.

Next came the riddle of technique. So deeply, fundamentally counter-intuitive. A drop knee, for instance – surely that makes you go lower, not higher? Spin and turn your back on the target hold – *what*? That makes no sense – *but my reach is now a metre further! I can make the next grip.* Wild!

In the early days I was constantly outwitted when onsighting. Lacked the skill to read the holds fast enough before I pumped out. Battled my way up, surviving on strength and panic. Recall asking a veteran climber friend how he did it, how he knew. But he just shrugged and said 'Time'. *Time?* Surely not! I needed to know immediately! So I concentrated harder. Picked up tips, piecemeal. Kept nibbling the crumbs.

After twenty years, I remain intellectually intrigued by the shapes and texture and structure of routes. Can still get shut down on an easy-looking finger-crack, misread sequences, mess up my feet. However much I learn and know, the puzzle can still surprise me and leave me bamboozled – flip-flapping on the ropes like an out-of-water mackerel.

But still I can't stop biting.

Excitement:
The Secret

'Do you want to know The Secret?' asks Trevor as he leans back majestically and clips the second bolt.

'Yes, yes!' I cry. 'Tell me The Secret! Tell me The Secret!'

Trevor smiles beatifically then infuriatingly returns to the climb, moving with serene grace. He clips the third bolt in an unhurried manner and, again, smiles down. If he were a mermaid he would be brushing his golden hair, tempting sailors onto the rocks.

'I have discovered The Secret,' he says, enigmatically.

'Tell me, tell me!' I shout, hopping up and down. 'Tell me The Secret!'

Trevor is drifting away now, heavenwards, but I need this information. Don't we all want The Secret? Show me the way to greater success, less strife, more creativity, heightened awareness, better sex with sexier people, spiritual contentment, happiness...

Trevor's at the top. I lower him down. We are on a level again.

'Tell me The Secret!' I implore him.

Trevor is still beaming. 'You know the way everyone always says "Keep your arms straight!", "Use your feet!"?'

'Yes, yes, Trevor, I do.'

'Especially for beginners? We say these things but then we don't really explain how it works,' he continues. 'But there's a missing link.'

'A missing link? What is it? Tell me! *Tell me!*'

He hands me the rope and I tie in automatically. I've had five hours' sleep. Trevor has just picked me up from the airport and now, perched far out in the Mediterranean, the high dome of the Peñón is turning rosy in the evening light.

I clean my shoes and step onto the limestone; the holds are crisp solution pockets, the wall inviting, textured, easy-angled. Within a move or two the flight, the parking headaches, the cancelled work and decision to abandon half-done tasks are all worth it, it's worth it to be here, even for this one climb, with the sky shifting neon at the witching hour, the sea at our backs and the birds starting to chorus.

I make a high step-up with my left toe. This is a signature move. I'm good at high step-ups, my hips are flexible, I'm proud of this skill. I stretch for tip-length razor holds and hoick up on them, pivoting my left knee, right leg lagging behind like a lazy eye. Even as I do this, I sense that I have done something out of kilter. Something in Trevor's silence. Something in the way the sky has turned orange.

I'm lowered down to the ground.

'Tell me The Secret, Trev. Please,' I mumble as I sit in the dust at his feet. Happily I've known Trev for several decades. Which means I don't need to maintain any show of dignity.

'At some point, most of us hit a limit,' sparkles Trevor, warming to the indirectness of his explanation, 'a plateau. And if we're keen, we work at getting beyond it. But, typically, we work at the wrong things! We try to get stronger, get fitter, get thinner and lighter.'

I unlace my shoes. I am painfully aware of how weak and unfit I am.

'But how many of us consciously work on our technique? Fitness and strength are fleeting and easily lost. But technique will stay with you forever.'

'Tell me, tell me!' I plead.

'Particularly once people have been climbing for a long time. Not many people keep looking at their technique after they've been climbing for years and years. They take it for granted, or get curiously insulted if you make any suggestions...'

'*Trev*,' I croak.

'...but top tennis players get coaching, world-class snooker players get coaching. Why should climbers be any different?'

'*Tell me The Secret!*'

Trevor is, by this time, fluidly ascending a 6c.

'The Secret is a basic sequence,' he reveals, cheerfully, over his shoulder, 'it's a template – the missing link that makes sense of the clichés we tell beginners. It's the way the really top climbers move if you study videos of the best of the best, both women and men.

'This is The Secret:

1. Using Leg A, *step onto a foothold.* Small steps are better than big steps, even if it means using smears or intermediaries rather than an obvious, high ledge;

2. *Lean sideways and down* over Leg A. By moving sideways and down, you make at least one arm straighten (straight arms like we tell beginners!). You can now put your full weight onto Leg A and be entirely in balance;

3. This releases Leg B. *Move Leg B up* onto a foothold, still with straight arms, your body relaxed, *keeping your core weight stationary;*

4. Now both feet are on holds, *push up with both legs.* Use the power in your legs for both momentum and direction. Your hands are only there to stabilise this movement.'

Trevor has been demonstrating The Secret. He carries on up with fluid, non-spectacular efficiency. I lower him down. We are silent for a little while. My pet style of high steps and a dragging back leg is likely to be obsolete. Any upward movement of the hips without both legs being on the rock pushing is probably poor technique. I'm going to have to think about this.

The sky by this time is a fantastical shocking pink. The Peñón beckons, peachy, a siren in the sea, the finest routes in Costa Blanca and still never climbed by me in all my trips out to Spain because I'd never brought a rack and never had two ropes. And maybe I'd been too intimidated. As night falls, we begin coiling the rope and putting the kit away.

Having come raw from the English winter with a mere handful of routes under my belt this year, how would my body deal with climbing day after day?

Flash forward to the end of the trip and, having concentrated on The Secret (okay, yes, and I also borrowed shoes with better edges!), I climbed all week at my best grade in a while, went up the Peñón twice, didn't have a rest day and didn't have torn tips, hurty arms or bloody nails.

And Trevor, nearing forty-nine though looking like he's in his thirties, is weaker than he was many years ago but climbing harder. Because his technique is better than it's ever been and still improving all the time. He led his first 8a+ last year and is aiming to lead his first 8b when he's fifty.

So that's The Secret. And a secret is still a secret if you don't tell too many people. Right?

Peacefulness:
Do Less

When coaching, one of my trademark phrases is *Do less*.

It is important to do less. There will be far too much to do down the line – tackle that overhang, another eighteen pitches – to waste your energy now. If you're not strong (and I'm not strong), it becomes even more important to do less. A fuller message might be *Do less and be smarter with where you put your effort*, or indeed *Do less and get more technical* or even *Do less and get more spiritual*. But more of that later. For the time being *Do less* is short enough to remember, and in the heat of the moment that might do the trick.

If you've just arrived at the bouldering gym, a nice start is to choose some huge handholds and okay foot placements, and dangle for a moment. How softly can you grip and still be hanging there? With each breath, how much tension can you drop through your neck, your shoulders, your elbows, your spine, your hips? Are you holding unnecessarily in your knees? Drop it down. Are you carrying weight in your heels? Let it go. *Do less.*

Put your consciousness in your feet. Non-climbers and new climbers often treat feet like heavy lumps. Blobs which weigh the legs down. But feet are alive; so much happens in secret inside those tight boots! Both velocity and direction come from the feet. Which is way, way easier on the arms and hands and the fingers. Fingers are tiny compared to legs. Help those tiny fingers do less!

Rest at every opportunity. If there is a big jug, a chance to bridge, a bit of back-and-footing, a jam – use it to rest. Swing to reach a hold, rather than pull – it's much less demanding. Often a defined part of your body will get sacrificed to pain. Select that isolated part – the left calf on a slab, the right fist in a jam – and focus on letting the tension slide from the rest of your body, especially from arms and hands. Encourage them to save themselves for later on in the climb when they might be needed to crank. Moment to moment, in as much of your body as you can – *do less*.

Learn better technique. Climbing skilfully helps you do more with less. Yank with your hands? No – pull in with that heel hook. Maintain that stress-position? No – let your free-flying limbs flag out and counterbalance. For beginners especially, better technique facilitates rapid improvements. But at any level, good technique allows you to punch above your weight. Johnny Dawes is the absolute legend of doing less. He was never 'fit' – but my God, what he climbed! And how he climbed it! Once it has seeped into your gut and your lungs and the balls of your feet, better technique will stay with you, as body memory. So if you get injured or are busy at work and can't climb for a few weeks, your fitness and strength will tumble. But good technique will still be there. Good technique will tuck in your rope bag like a little slinky cat.

A similar approach works wonders with gear. Do less! Be calm with the ropes and they're inclined to behave and run smoothly. As a trad second, brutal handling can embed the kit deeper, damage wires and lose cams. Learn to cajole runners out gently. With stubborn placements, try the Look-away Trick: gaze absolutely anywhere apart from at the piece in question and let your mind wander whilst fingers and rock negotiate an outcome. Many times this abstracted, non-confrontational approach has borne fruit. Yanking and tugging might do the job as a last resort – but are not the first port of call.

Do less with your mind. Let it rest. There are tips elsewhere in the climbing canon about getting 'in the zone'. Clearing your mind of rubbish (end-gaining, targets, performance anxiety, everyday worries) leaves more space to focus on the puzzle, the movement, the rock.

Likewise, do less with your emotions. Climbing can be a wonderful place to channel and transform all sorts of difficult feelings – sadness, anger, frustration, irritation. Let all those feelings go. Play on the rock, become absorbed in limestone, involved in granite, occupied by grit, distracted by plastic. Climb. Let your heart relax. *Do less*.

What happens if you don't push yourself all the time?

If you don't work your weaknesses? Don't train? Quite possibly, you are now free to have a great time on the rock or the wall, climbing comfortably, climbing a lot, climbing for pleasure, climbing lovely things. The irony is that your grade may go up too. Because effort isn't the only driver – there are many others, and my favourite is desire. When you're really hooked by a line or obsessed with a project, then you'll build your skill-set and you'll tackle the route with gusto – commit yourself utterly to that stunning F6b+ or that bewitching E4. Desire is powerful and fearless. Desire is effortless! Why force yourself?

This whole *Do less* thing, I realise, is a luxury. I know if you're on the breadline, a refugee, a single parent on benefits, the *Do less* construct will come across as blithe and privileged. If you're struggling, then *Do less* may not be the correct way to keep your head above water. But I imagine (because you have paid money for an artsy, feminist book on a hobby) that the majority of people reading will have a certain amount of physical, financial and cultural capital, some of which they can choose to conserve.

As I say, this is a partial philosophy. Add it to the mix. It suits me, I guess, because by habit and personality type, I tend to try too hard. *Do less* is a quick reminder.

Art of the Rest

'Fiddlesticks!' Squirrel Nutkin didn't mince his words. Same place every time! He hung, exasperated, beneath the crux of an indoor 6a+. The route was his nemesis and time was running out before it disappeared forever. It took a devious line up a groove and had been set by the Colossus in one of his distinctly curmudgeonly moods. Awkward, delicate, obscure, a distillation of decades of trad climbing matured by decades of barely going outdoors at all. Like a painting from memory, it held the soul of a multitude of climbs.

'Any tips?' Squirrel Nutkin appealed. This wasn't my forte. I tried to do what I'd heard other folks do. Called up, 'Okay! Right hand to the / reach over, no! Um! That's it! Now move your left foot – outside edge, outside edge! Try / um...!' Well, that speaks for itself. So then I climbed it. I thought that might be clearer. I repeated the hard section in the middle to be helpful but made a mess of it and couldn't remember the sequence and went up it two different ways, one attractive, one ugly. Not helpful, no.

So then, in the end, I communicated what I really meant: 'Don't try and go up it! If there's a big handhold and you usually rush past, then pause for a moment. If you get confused and then tend to flop off, try and get in balance instead. Get comfy and relax. Look around! Don't try to go up!' Welcome to the reverse psychology of anti-ambition: the Art of the Rest.

I mentioned this approach to Sandstorm a while later. Whilst new to climbing, she had intuitively grasped the concept: 'You've got to spot the breaks,' she said. 'Small ones might be an espresso. A full hands-off rest might be a cappuccino with a slice of carrot cake.' Exactly, I say. Quite so.

On real rock the key is to take rests when you can. And, to fully clarify, by 'rest' I mean the technical rest, recovering while still on the climb, not going off-route and not weighting the rope or the gear. Opportunistic and deliberate: taking stock on an incut handhold, shaking out on a smeared bridge, a heel-hook round a block, a cheeky knee-bar.

And 'rest' of course is relative. On an overhanging, short, fierce route, taking it in turns to hang right-hand, left-hand, right-hand, left-hand at a stupid steep angle is the rest. Isolation of parts is crucial, so one part of your body gets sacrificed to pain. Calves screaming murder on a tiny slate overlap whilst you chalk up slowly, at ease. Stricken fingers pinched white on crystal dinks while you breathe softly into your stomach, your quiet feet. Left-hand fingers torqued in the agony of a sharp-sided limestone pocket leaving your right hand dangling, floppy and loose, the roll through your shoulders and down your spine fluid and easy like rosary beads without the guilt.

But how is any progress made? Look up. It's a puzzle! Layback or jam? And what's that? A jug or a flattie? Best approach it static, only slap if I have to. What happens if I twist the other way? Or match? Curiosity draws me upwards. Solving the puzzle. And yes of course, in the back of my mind, that driving desire to finish the route clean. But keep that in check. Only let it out when the big guns are needed.

For some caveats are necessary here. Clearly there's a place for the all-out thrutching ghastly face of effort – giving it some welly through a roof and so forth. And it goes without saying that I'm no pure exponent of anti-ambition. Far from it! Given half a chance I'm heaving needlessly, bent-armed on crimps or smashing my hands up on cracks with no decent excuse. I just wanted to step back and celebrate the siege tactic of peacefulness.

I suspect the concept of resting has become steadily obsolete, superseded in the context of indoor roped walls and outdoor sport climbing and the new, cheerful culture of GriGris and redpoints. Why rest when you can forge straight up and take a big lob? Why rest when you can just hang on the rope? Resting is old-fashioned now, a traditional artform. Underwhelming, perhaps, like needlepoint or patchwork, not as glamorous as architecture or as impressive as statues in bronze but a lovely skill nonetheless.

Sometimes I wonder if I've taken it a bit far. Many's the time that I've driven to Pembroke or the north coast of Devon and just pulled up the van and looked out to sea; made tea on the little stove and lain with the sliding door open and the sun beaming in or, more likely, with the door ajar and the rain battering; watching small figures walking up to the surf, heads bowed; listening to the wind in the whipping grass and the far crash of the waves on the shore. It's the idea of just being somewhere and not really doing anything.

Does that make me a massive loser? For there's a value system here. Being somewhere is seen as less valuable than conquering something. Stillness in our culture is seen as a waste of time. Lack of ambition in a career as lack of competence. Taking a little nap in the middle of the day is seen as a weakness.

Where was I? Ah, yes. Wandering back past the 6a+. Squirrel Nutkin had moved through the crux and was hanging on the rope just above it. So that was splendid; the furthest he'd ever got in one push. 'Great!' I shout, scanning the groove for rests. Those screw-ins were at least a plastic beaker of squash.

'Bridge out!'

VEHEMENCE

Vehemence:
Glory of Movement

Dance

Sea cliffs prompt somatic
Fabulousness. A private show

Flamenco, some kind of ballet
In a theatre after-hours

Green room empty, boards bare
No audience. You take the hand

Of the rock and slide and sweep
From placement to placement

Bodyweight in a spin
Around the pinpoint of your tight

Rubber toe. The fatal dance
Where you can let yourself go

Clash

Crew! Bridge out and fist jam
Indeed, no! Boots chest-height
and layback!

That clash when the mind has a plan
Whilst your flesh
Has different ideas

Like an old fashioned frigate
With the sails set for running
Helmed into the wind

The grey stuff playing captain
Stepping in to take charge
Give orders

But muscle and bone
Are stroppy. Will refuse
To do what they're told. Will mutiny

Who wins? Usually one
Or the other
And then you get a bit higher

But a stalemate?
Then you're stuck in irons
The least fun

Is the on-board shoot-out
Body and brain at opposite ends of the deck
Both with guns

Genius

Indoors or outdoors, climbing demonstrates
The visceral intelligence of matter

Not brain-thinking, rather
A logic from the belly. Minuscule re-adjustments

Counter-balancing, an abacus of limbs
Where physical conundrums are crunched

Understood and acted upon. But so fast!
The body is a genius

Carnal brilliance as your frame factors in
Distance, size, reliability, song

And shifts until, at best, you embody
A barbarian mix

Of maths and music and war and homeliness
With the probability of keeping you safe

Slingshot

A game of falling up
Casting your body
From one notch to the next

Swinging in arcs
Some sort of physics
Momentum flicking you to the top

That astounding feeling
Of being suspended, mid-move, in air
The twanging core

Lobbing your bulk in a rockover
One hip to the other
Being caught by the holds

Or the unhinged whip
As your free limbs fling out
To counter a manoeuvre. Weight

Triggering a reflex to grip
Gravity in tension
With pleasure and ambition

Forces which yank you back then
Hurl you up the route
Like a slingshot

Commitment:
Slopers

We meet at the front desk. Strangers. I've seen his booking form, appreciated his line in understatement. 'What do you believe your current strengths are?' 'None in particular'. New to bouldering, a desire to learn respectable habits from the beginning. 'Your biggest weakness?' 'Large, rounded grips'.

Initially, we warm up, talk about other skills, practise other techniques, play on different sections of the wall – but really we both know, it's all about those large, rounded grips. They eye us from the plywood – so enormous! So colourful! So untenable. Are they mocking us? Doubtless. But mesmerising! Truly, there's nothing so enticing as a marginal sloper which you sense, at gut level, you might stick.

'Hang on that,' I suggest, gesturing towards a giant, orange half-world. He rushes up, falls. Wrong! That really is no way to approach this kind of voluptuousness. Grabbing and squeezing? No, no, no.

Climb from the heart. Here. Approach slower. Feel the hold. Be expansive. Widen the breadth of your palm, soften your skin, relax into the resin so your pores meld with the grain. Emanate all the love in your being to this rounded, moulded dome. Become weak at the knees. Buckle. Keep your feet low. Hang loose. Let your arms graze the paintwork, until you're lying vertically together on this bed of ply. Like you don't want to be anywhere else. As if you'll stay there forever. Commit.

He softens. Drops his weight. Crumples like a supplicant, a suitor. He doesn't hold the plastic. The sloper holds him. And so the passion begins.

After a while he becomes comfortable – familiar and steady on the hold that originally had no time for him at all. His hands embrace the roundedness, secure and stable. A family man, almost. When he tries to move up and left to the next orange sloper, he is spat off immediately. No wonder! He yanked at it. Plus he clearly revealed his infidelity, his intention to defect. A double whammy.

Slopers, out of all the hold-types, seem the most possessive. Buckets can't wait for you to leave – watch the speed with which people romp along rows of jugs. The strenuousness of laybacks makes a rapid up-down-or-off inevitable. But slopers aren't that keen on sharing.

So how can you move on? Be kind, I advise. But also a little sneaky. Have a plan. Execute it cleanly. Change comes from your feet – the direction, distance and speed of the shift. Be accurate. It's no use plonking your toe anywhere on this orange mini-ledge – see the nobble here, half an inch higher? And this ridge towards the edge? Choose that, it means you triangulate a very, very minor slab. Use the angles. As to your hands, make every touch count, even the last – especially the last! – leave a positive memory, a tenderness. Never leave with a fight. No one likes that. Push up. And at the eleventh hour, go to the next sloper, and commit to that, with all your heart.

He's moving now as if he means it. I step back. It's gorgeous, this – the start of something beautiful. I hope it lasts. I think it will. He seems a nice lad.

Hurt:
Aren't You the Climber?

The ordinary world bored me to death. It was so obvious, laid out on a plate like a cheap ploughman's – floppy lettuce, mass-produced chutney and stale bread. Unfortunately, shoulder problems had put a stop to my climbing and I'd been left picking at this dreary day-to-day life, pushing the food around with my fork. After a while I resorted to jogging to give my failing body something to do. One particular blustery day rounding a rise in a city park, a stranger's face lit up. She called out, 'Aren't you the climber?'

Now, this would have been baffling at any point as I'm not in any way famous or well known. But coming as it did then, after eighteen months without touching rock, in the unguarded rut of an identity crisis, it span me into utter confusion. What to say? I skimmed her glance and smiled off-kilter and skittered away all a-dither.

Who was I if I didn't climb? I scampered on, till my thighs smouldered and lungs burned at the edges. With each foot-fall the question stabbed me like a skewer – who, indeed, was I if I didn't climb? Climbing wasn't a bit of sport to me! Climbing had been my lifestyle, my survival kit, my mental health, my purpose, my love.

Ran on, head down, through a scrubby backfield. A while
back, just beside the path here, I'd rumbled a couple of
guys stripping plastic from lengths of stolen cable. Crossing
a footbridge, followed a stretch next to the pond where
the swans once nested so that inadvertently, whatever
the season, I'd always scan for grey fluffballs of cygnets.
Picking up speed, continued past the tatty tree where I'd
once gathered elderflowers for cordial. These memories
emerged, one by one, place by place, each a neat, discrete
recollection.

As I got into my stride, pacing the high fields parallel to
the motorway, I started thinking about Pembroke. It would
be a lovely day in Pembroke, bright and breezy with high
clouds wisping in from the north. The sort of day, even
now, to park up beyond Bosherston and stroll along the
cliff-top. And this is the thing: memories there are an
entirely different creature. Not the ordinary doings of the
everyday world. No. A fairytale zone of epics and heroics
populated by goblins and monsters; a weird and wonderful
multi-layered remembering where fantastical deeds and
people and experiences are jumbled together and embedded in my heart and my limbs and the landscape.

Still in Pembroke, walk a hundred metres east of the
car-park. The litany of names echoes already: Army
Dreamers, Poisoned Arrow, Zodiac, Kraken; a whispering
of myths. Listen! The thunder of ludicrous waves as spume

pitches over the walls; the music of metalware; the gulls. Look! A swirl of glitter and dust, kaleidoscope of images: perfect grey holds, sun on my left shoulder, bomber nut slots, makeshift quickdraws from a harness entirely cleared of gear, laybacking wildly, rapid down-climbing not quite saving the fall, red tat of a miraculous Friend 5, round rock-pools. The scene of my alarming first ever abseil under the tutelage of the Firestarter. Leading Deranged in the zone when it all came together. Five adults and a child in a pop-up baby-tent by the stakes, gulping champagne from the bottle and eating birthday cake as the squall turned nasty. Lundy, sometimes as clear as an upside-down frying pan, sometimes seemingly not there at all. Memories that aren't even mine: White Rhino tumbling with legs astride the knife of The Butcher; Puss-in-Boots smashing his heels on the same route. A late summer outing with King of Kings, running across the grass in bare feet, fully racked up, red sun already dipping on the watery horizon.

The rush of associations arises unbidden, merged together like smells from a kitchen: choc chip cookies, roast chicken, coffee and peppermint – overlapping and splendid; a quiet insistent clamouring, like hunger. And there it is. Nothing is lost. The hours and days and years spent in that short section of British coast are still there, ripening like mature cheese. Like good wine.

Which is why, like a non-drinking alcoholic, I'm still a climber. And why, when I die, my ashes will be scattered over the cliffs at St Govan's. So much of me is there already.

By now I'm thumping through the underpass towards Tesco and Ikea. I don't seem to have noticed the last two miles. But it doesn't matter. It doesn't matter that I'm injured. It doesn't matter that I'm stuck in the city. I feel reconciled in my particles of flesh, my molecules of sinew. I know what to answer. My trainers pound the tarmac in a familiar mantra: *I'm a climber – I'm a climber – I'm a climber.*

Pain:
Salt

For most of us in the west, our lives are geared around comfort. Like slugs, don't we recoil from salt? This makes sense. But is not enough.

Pain is a funny thing. Pain is used in meditation to promote focus, to pull the mind away from trivia. Pain can illuminate habits and repetitions. Pain can be followed as a road map through hang-ups and deep-seated trauma. Pain is a language, a way of passing on information without words. A wide vocabulary is best – lexicon of good pain and bad pain and many pains in between like Inuit descriptions of snow. Not running away from pain is counter-intuitive, but a helpful talent. Clinics in pain management oftentimes aren't trying to rid people of pain, but to encourage open communication. Certain sports – like road cycling and cold water swimming – are famous for pain and pain thresholds and moving through and beyond pain. There are many aspects to pain. It is a skill in itself. Isolation of parts (an excruciating left forearm whilst you clip, the rest of your body determinedly relaxed), belaying in a T-shirt at the freezing apex of the cliff, legs and arms numb with cold. What to do? Nothing to be done. Sit with the pain. It will end.

This sort of pain, the right amount of pain, feels queerly good. Nourishing. A body-reboot. A re-baptism. A dip in the salty sea by moonlight.

Bewilderment:
Past the Peak

Uncertainty tugged at me like a querulous dog. Chewed the slippers in the hall. Upset my peace and disturbed my sleep. What had become of that irreligious zeal? The unreasonable conviction that as long as I was climbing – sea-cliff trad, multipitch, sport, bouldering for an hour over at Bonehill on a winter's day – I knew I was doing the right thing.

It created so much more time, not climbing. An oil-slick of hours on which to slip up. Have you noticed how a walk takes forty-five minutes but climbing takes all day? Ditto a game of badminton. Ditto playing the guitar. The leftover time gained a toxic quality.

How to use it all up? I tried experimenting with everyday pleasures. Which is how I came to be sitting mildly in the Cross-Country carriage, window seat, front-facing, idly tracing the canals past Bath, marvelling at the expanse of Birmingham, leafing *The Guardian*, toying with pebbles of letters in my mind: *Romantically naïve – on the verge of tears (4,4)*; *All bothered and bewildered (2,3)*; *Beekeeper (8)*. I purchased tea from the refreshments trolley. It was a lovely journey made hazardous with confusion. In the old days I'd have driven up late at night, hour after hour without stops, music loud, outside lane, coffee and Bounty bars because in the old days the daytimes were precious as I knew what to do in them.

Bothered and bewildered, ending in 'a'. The irony was that I wasn't even injured any more. The wild goose chase of hospitals, physio, osteo, operations which had finally fixed my body had left my head floundering. Stripped of faith, I no longer understood the rituals of browsing guidebooks and belaying in the shade on a sunny day. Having been in love for many years, hopelessly, deliciously in love, my passion for the rock had abruptly stopped, my Bottom was suddenly a donkey, the thought of leading Dream Of White Horses left me numb.

But I wasn't sure. What had been lost? The Days of Glory. The cauterising moments of sanctity when you commit to a trail of poor gear on the Culm Coast and Puss-in-Boots is miles below and the only option at all in the wide world is to ascend higher and higher and your feet are prayers on the tiny overlaps and the hole in the top of your head blasts up to heaven in a white beam of fear and the fear gobbles up everything but the minute breeze on your left temple and the poor fingerlock and the stir of the sea and there is no doubt that you are absolutely alive and each cell in your body is tingling with it.

The connecting service worked fine and by early afternoon I'd alighted at the tiny station at Hathersage. I walked along the little lane to wait by the main road and sat on a bin. Only climbers would sit on a bin, I thought.

A white van pulled up piled chocka with insulation offcuts. 'I'm going to line the cellar!' Alma Mater called out. 'Just haven't got round to it. Van's been like this for weeks! Let's go to Stanage!' *Stanage.* My heart shrank involuntarily, salt in a wound, like bumping into an ex at a social event. I squeezed in shotgun between the offcuts and the baby and Alma Mater steered us off into the countryside.

Bouldering in the Peak can appear awfully unappealing when you don't climb anymore. The sky a sweep of low grey stratus. Erosion bunkers beneath the boulders pooling with tacky mud. The rock green and dark from days of rain. Surely a late lunch in the Scotsman's Pack was a better idea? I still had form with a good steak and ale pie. I traipsed in Alma Mater's footprints up along the winding path. Incredibly it seemed to me, given the uninspiring afternoon, the easy boulders were being assaulted on all sides by teams of ambitious young people with logoed beanies; their multiple mats made each boulder resemble a Christmas tree surrounded by large presents. I felt a tad bah-humbuggy.

We sat down. Alma Mater took Squidge out of the papoose. The hard, damp outcrop sloped at a miserable angle. I had no inclination whatsoever to climb. I clutched Squidge like a hot-water bottle whilst Alma Mater waltzed up a couple of problems. Glancing to my left I clocked a highball bloc, also surrounded by people. They were working a problem that I remembered doing. I didn't see anyone top out. Partly I felt proud of what I'd once done. Simultaneously I felt crushed that I couldn't possibly do it now. Laurels or exile? It's a tricky one.

'Do this one, then that one, then that one,' commanded Alma Mater, 'Right to left.' She had so little sympathy with my woebegone condition, it's almost as if she hadn't noticed it. She whisked Squidge away, which left me few options. I crowbarred the cold rock-boots on, one of Cinderella's Sisters (how were they so tiny?), tip-toed across the slimy stepping stones, sprang onto an abandoned mat and teetered onto the rock.

It was immediately beautiful. My body changed. Breathing slowed. A radical non-intellectual, non-cerebral shift. Right foot anchored to the dimple of grit, hand stretched up to the sloping pocket, bodymass dipping to the heel of my palm, right hip dropping down; left foot up and, again, that utter transfer of weight, like lobbing a ball, tossing a basket of eggs, throwing your heart to the man you love, hoping he'll catch it.

Super-hearing suddenly. Taste of the air. A monumental expanse in my brain momentarily relieved of the petty cacophony of grocery shopping, doctor's appointments, social paranoia that I said the wrong thing to the woman in the car park, replacing her worn front offside tyre. It's still there. My capacity to fall head over heels. To believe.

Shortly after this, a shower came over. We armoured up once more in layers of fleece and waterproofs and continued along the crest of the Edge. The landscape reverted to greys and sombre greens. Who'd have thought it? Of all the crags for a south-west lass – the dour Dark Peak!

Dependency:
Antidepressant Sun Pills

Day after day it rains. Anxiety, tension headaches, a malaise I can't place. A lostness, like I have a razor in my hand and feel sure it's good for something, but can't remember what. My heart, heaving and swirling in my chest, has gathered all the blood from my body. It is a reservoir threatening to burst its banks. My face is drained.

Make plans for a single pitch route at the Gorge this afternoon. A half-window, between storms. Drive down. Get out. Ropes on the wet grass, brambles and roadside litter. Familiar flake-line, steep but good gear. Put my hands on the rock, medication by touch, press down and become absorbed. Let the waters recede. Become calm.

Before climbing, I never used to be so weather-dependent. But before climbing, I had very few mechanisms for emotional regulation. Now the weather is my Big Pharma, my physician.

Please Doctor, prescribe a dry spell! And an extra-large blister-pack of sun.

COMPASSION

Compassion:
Un-doing Dominance

Do we function by these hierarchies?

E5 over VS;
Summit over foothills;
Grades over enjoyment;
Words (speech) over silence (listening);
Doing (to) over being (with);
Human over non-human (we can drill the cliff, it doesn't mind, it doesn't have feelings).

Fear:
Beauty and the Beast

It is all about the beast of fear.

Cauterising terror that strips all dross away and leaves you vivid. Where each inhalation and out-breath is a miracle. Texture of rock between left thumb and two fingers, the pinch, exquisite in its lucidity. Wire six feet below you, a so-so flared placement, shallow cam very far below that. Fifteen metres to the deck, up-pointing shards of slate. Test the crimps up and right, smooth the rock with tips. Gamble on gear at the next break, it looks like there might be a slot but you can't be sure. Poor foothold, knee-height, a coin-width overlap, raise your toes gently, a last intake of oxygen and cast your weight and now you can't reverse and you can't get off, no one can help you, no one can drop a rope, you are on lead and your mind is one hundred per cent gripped and your body is incandescent with life.

And therein lies the beauty.

Fearlessness:
A Double-edged Sword

Non-climbers often think climbers aren't scared. Not so! Climbing is terrifying. Many of us climb to the limit of our fear-tolerance, rather than to the edge of our technical ability. Fear is what we are exploring, touching, negotiating, playing with, handling.

In *Free Solo*, brain scans demonstrate that Alex Honnold does not have a normally functioning amygdala. Typical fear-triggers do nothing for him. He does not feel it. He does not bathe in the wash of terror as most people do. A number of high-performing athletes I know seem to share this characteristic. So they cave dive, they BASE jump, they wing-suit, they solo. Are they trying to feel what others feel, climbing a Very Severe? To feel something?

Culturally, there is a celebration of the defect of fearlessness.

Invisibility:
Older Woman at the Base of the Crag

We are standing at the base of the crag. It is my local crag, I have climbed here for years, I know all the routes off by heart, I know which accidents have happened here, I know the history of politics around bolting, I know which aspect it faces, which parts get sunshine in different seasons, due to tree-cover or the rotation of the earth or the sun's height at midday in December compared to June. I know how the rock feels on a warm day and which routes dry quickest after rain. There are five of us, we came in two carloads, and have met up. I am fifty-one. I have white-grey hair which is tied in a plait half-way down to my waist. The others are much younger than me, in years. One is learning to belay, the other four are competent-to-good, but still inexperienced outdoors. Three of them are my friends, the others friends-of-friends, a mix of women and men. We are gathered, they all turn to me, one asks, 'What routes are here?' and I start to tell them the routes. The crag is quite busy. A man in an adjacent group, who we do not know, turns away from his climbing partner and starts listing out the routes, with large hand gestures. He talks right over me. I carry on talking and for a few moments we are both talking simultaneously about the routes at the crag. He is louder than me. After a while I stop answering the question. Perhaps he didn't hear me. Perhaps he didn't see me at all. All my friends and climbing cohort have turned to him and are listening to him tell them about the routes.

Exclusion:
The Perfect Line

'My intuitions lie with freedom of speech over policing/
regulation. I guess there are some examples that cross
the line but I don't know where that line is. Who does
know where that line is? And who gets to decide where
the line is?'

Hazel Findlay, 2019

The stack of vintage magazines beside the circuit boards
is always worth a browse. So much has changed! So little
has changed! The outfits. The hardware. The destinations,
always looking wonderful, over the years. Flicking through.
Eyes caught by a full page photo. Mali, West Africa. Black-
skinned youth in dirty trousers leaning against the sandstone. Dwarfed by spray-painted European route names.
There is a short caption, by Ray Wood. It concludes, 'Leaving [the environmental] issue aside however, assuming you
have the right to paint the name of a route at the bottom in
bright yellow paint has a ring of colonialism about it.' The
date of the magazine is November 2003. In the intervening

years, how much has the conversation moved on?

There are complex issues connected to new routing. Who gets to do what, and where? How powerful is a name? What has been the impact of the current system? What could be better? Nowadays there is much greater awareness of sexism, racism, cultural imperialism and so on. How should we integrate this knowledge into climbing, into new routing? On the other hand, one of the beauties of climbing, to my mind, is its lawlessness. It is quite unregulated. We go where we like, put our lives in danger, clamber about rock faces all over the place willy-nilly. It's great. I baulk at imposing restrictions or codes of practice. But maybe we should?

It's a tricky conversation. The trouble is, there is no simple correct answer. We're all looking for the Perfect Line. But that line can be smudged, chalked, rubbed out and redrawn depending on myriad factors including personality, gender, location, faith and time. In this article I'll consider culture and naming in the UK before moving on to look at new routing abroad.

The Cultural Dominance of White Guys

For the past hundred years and more, UK tradition has decreed that whoever climbs it first gets to name the route. They have free rein and can choose whatever name they like. This name and description then get preserved in guidebooks. This practice is not God-given, or sacrosanct, or the Truth; it is just one way. A way which, it must be said, is fairly popular worldwide. But nonetheless it is not the only way, and it is not inevitable.

A conspicuous issue for me, regarding this naming and claiming convention, is the cultural dominance of white guys. Read the 'historical' sections of guidebooks. Over and over again I end up gazing at lists and biographies and photos of white men. Which has repercussions. When one demographic (in this case white, male) monopolises a scene, it has the effect of homogenising the climbing environment. It inevitably excludes others, who are not white men. It sends out the message that *this place is not for you*. Not meaning to, but it does. So I can feel alienated and miffed. Feel the ghosts of women past, suffocated by skirts and convention, who could have been great first ascensionists but never had the chance. Feel conflicted, because admiration and envy are also in there. As I said in the introduction, this is not a straightforward debate.

Knowing the rebelliousness of traditional climbers – misfits! mass-trespassers! – how galling for such guys, how objectionable, to be associated with 'patriarchy', with white, male presumption, with the establishment. How did that happen? How did poacher turn game-keeper? Or, more accurately, see how they co-exist – rebel, misogynist, husband, dirtbag, lover, bully. We all wear many hats.

I also get it, that new-routers are the ones who invest their time and knowledge into putting up new lines. Can admire the pioneering spirit, discomfort, tolerance of risk, especially in ground-up trad. The vision! Appreciate the financial cost and equipment and dedication needed in developing new sport crags. Nevertheless, doesn't this sometimes slip into smash-and-grab? A sort of feeding frenzy to 'bag' the best lines. All those stories of 'stealing' routes, bad/rushed bolting and fabricated ascents. Greed. And isn't it generated by this system? I'm not all against greed, per se. Greed is close to desire, and I'm a big fan of desire. On the other hand, gluttony and lust are both Deadly Sins. So shouldn't some care be taken, lest we go to hell?

Simply the idea of being able to claim and name pieces of rock resonates with presumption. A recent Canadian article notes the response from one female interviewee: 'Lilith said that she would never feel entitled to name […] a cliff…' (Wigglesworth, 2019). But, both historically and nowadays, it seems men have felt thus entitled. And so this conquering and pioneering has gendered elements. Have men been, mainly, doing the conquering?

Well, why don't you get up and do it yourself then, Sarah-Jane, if you care so much? Yes, indeed, why don't I? Well, because it's scary and loose and slow and there is too much unknown for me (talking on-sight trad here). And regarding sport crags, I don't fancy the discomfort of hanging in a harness for hours, the noise of the drill, days spent with a wrecking bar when I could be out climbing. So am I a hypocrite? Maybe. I'm just saying how I feel.

As an aside, and in the interests of full disclosure, I did put up a new route once, when I got hopelessly lost and led a fresh line. My partner and I claimed it and named it Shaggy Dog Stories. I was excited. Can feel the thrill now, of telling people, encouraging them to try it and grade it and corroborate – or otherwise – our assessment of stars. Finding a name that made sense in context. It was so fun. I can see exactly how it would get addictive. Even that terminology implies the need for treatment. Enough said. Moving on.

Redressing the Balance?

Is this situation fixed, so nothing can be done? I'm not so sure. Like any history, these are selected facts, fore-grounded facts. Presentation and editing continue to shape our experience. For example, it was a relief for me when guidebooks downplayed the history sections. Then I could just crack on with the climbing. Also, many of the old black-and-white photos do feature women – but often very little is said about them. Perhaps more effort could be made here. Beyond guidebooks, an opus such as Ken Wilson's 1970s *Hard Rock* featured no articles by women. But contemporary anthologies really can do better, can make an active effort to recruit material from a more diverse base. If there isn't a significant proportion from non-white-male contributors in your selected essay book – why not? Because these people have been climbing. They will have stories.

As I said, new routing is not for me. But happily, I do not represent 'All Women'. So maybe now is the time to set about purposefully widening the field, so a greater range of people put up routes. Over twenty-five per cent of climbers, according to the BMC, are women now. There are many girls coming up in the sport. So shouldn't the aim be for a quarter of new routes to be female-led? For diverse new routers to have access to tools and equipment and training. To feel they can name. Should more effort and funding be directed towards such investment? This could be on every level, from individual activists passing on their knowledge to non-white-male enthusiasts, to increased support from the BMC, clubs and sponsors.

Is this pie in the sky? There is so little unclaimed rock left in Britain (more of that later), so has the horse bolted (so to speak), would this be tokenism, divvying up crumbs? Plus I realise my position is rife with contradiction. That I'm dubious about naming and claiming at all, philosophically; it conflicts with my call for women and other under-represented groups to put up more routes. In addition, setting up a binary of 'men' and 'women' sits badly with me – it is simplified, flawed, as I see gender as more nuanced and fluid. And besides, 'men' are not the enemy. These are my climbing partners, my friends. The perfect line wavering, meandering, zig-zagging. More like a scribble. A scribble of ideas.

The Power of a Name

What about the names themselves? Why does it matter? I appreciate we are all different, that names won't have the same impact on everyone. For myself, I am interested in language, and the symbolic (and actual) power of words. Naming is not peripheral to me, not a meaningless add-on. It gives a flavour to the whole area, to the whole route, the whole experience. In the wider cultural context, white, British men have named buildings and roads and stars and plants after themselves and each other and we all have to walk around and write addresses and orientate ourselves in the midst of this hubris. At the same time, there is a long, inglorious precedent of women, and people of colour, being written out of history, and their contributions minimised. Naming matters.

I'm not advocating chucking all the babies out with this dirty water. I'd like to celebrate the marvellousness of some nomenclature. On occasion, particularly in trad, the name of the route is so good it ferments the mystique. Like countless others, I wanted to climb A Dream of White Horses for many, many years before I made it to Wen Slab. Yes, I knew it was a classic line – but what a name! RIP, Ed Drummond. I also adore crags where generations of new routers have riffed with the theme. So on the military range in Pembroke, amongst a regiment of others, we have Army Dreamers, Front Line (the first buttress to face the sea! Hats off to that namer), Space Cadet (steep, so you would fall into space! HATS OFF!). These fill me with delight.

On the other hand, sometimes names miss the mark or are downright toxic. Names, intended to be light-hearted, edgy or funny to the namer, may be offensive, grating and rude to someone else. And when that 'someone else' is of a less powerful cultural demographic (female, Black, gay, disabled) then I'd suggest it is a pretty poor name. There are plenty of slightly (or very) racist and slightly (or very) misogynist route names in Britain. I began my climbing adventures in Devon, an area not known for its racial diversity. The local crag, Chudleigh, has a route called Wogs. I was shocked then and I'm shocked now. I can't believe it's still in the guidebooks. As to sexist names, just this week I was browsing the South Wales sport guide and came across Campaign for See-through Bikinis. Not the worst, but disrespectful and laddish. Last weekend I was leading just along from Menopausal Discharge. Hello? This is not purely a UK phenomenon. In Kalymnos, the one easy route at the back of the wildly overhanging Grande Grotta is called, condescendingly, Happy Girlfriend. Or how about climbing Tampon Applicator and She Got Drilled in Calabogie, Canada? Start looking out for inappropriate names; they're out there. They're everywhere.

How do you imagine women and/or people of colour feel about being at these crags, climbing these routes, reading these guidebooks? Would they feel welcome, respected, part of the in-joke? An insider? Or are they being told this joke is not for them, this route is not for them, this crag is not for them, this sport is not for them? And, clearly, the linguistic landscape would be different, more various, more unexpected if more diverse people did the naming. What names are not being told, not being heard?

Aside from outright insult, another feature to look out for is a stylised machismo in route names – Driller King, Sport Wars! Such names have so little to do with the landscape, and so much to do with assertions of masculinity. Would you want to tackle a route called, say, Cute Fluffy Kittens or Glittery Nail Varnish? They're equally silly, but they stand out as ridiculous, as we're not used to a hyper-feminised labelling. A little off-putting? Remember that feeling! For that is how I feel.

Other Ways and Other Names

There could be methods other than naming-by-the-first-ascensionist. It is possible. Just because we're used to one mechanism doesn't mean it's the only way or the best way. It's just the one with which we're familiar. The current way seems peculiarly British somehow – that winner-takes-all, first-past-the-post mentality. Planting a flag. Staking ownership. As an alternative method, names could be given by local schoolchildren, by nearby residents, by poets, by vote, by online competitions. No end of possibilities! And what might the impact of this be? If individual glory (naming and claiming) was bypassed, as well as expanding naming potential, would this alter the nature of new-routing? Would the avid drive to grab routes soften a little? The scales tip back to desire? Perhaps there could be a naming oversight committee, made up of diverse peoples in the climbing community, eight per cent Asian, four per cent Black, at least fifty per cent women – in line with the UK population. Why not?

And what to do about currently offensive names? Guidebook writers make efforts from time to time: one description of Happy Girlfriend notes the route is also suitable for happy boyfriends; embarrassed disclaimers accompany Wogs. Such awareness is appreciated. But can't the names themselves be changed? Rewriting history is always uncomfortable, but history is usually uncomfortable for someone (and frequently not the victor). In Sweden certain offensive route names were retrospectively banned and altered (Ward, 2010). Is it worth renaming grossly offensive routes? Or should we, as a community, sit with our shame?

New-routing Imperialism

As Ray Wood observed in the opening paragraph, isn't there a whiff of colonialism in putting up lines abroad – a new-routing imperialism?

It's easy to see why Brits seek new lines outside the UK. There is a shortage of virgin, native rock. British climbers started tackling peaks and cracks and grooves over a century ago. Save the odd hard eliminate, most peach lines are gone. These days, new routes on our islands are frequently bolted, on tiny crags and outcrops dug out from mud and ivy in forgotten, shattered quarries which used to be overlooked as hopeless but are now appreciated as grist for the mill.

So it seems that many British new-routers are putting up lines beyond these shores. Unclaimed rock! Cherries to pick! But this is also occurring in a particular context. Many of these locations are less economically privileged. We know our backstory of colonialism, imperialism, our involvement in the transatlantic slave trade, the Elgin Marbles, our taking without asking. Isn't it a little like going on safari and shooting big game, because we've killed all our own tigers and elephants? The routes get named with English references, English in-jokes, English language. Plus routes must surely have been named and claimed by westerners, over the years, that actually had earlier, undocumented, indigenous ascents. It makes me feel uncomfortable. How to square this relentless claiming and naming with respect for local rock, local people, the local climbing population?

The British have done plenty of inappropriate naming. Countries on other continents (Rhodesia after the white supremacist Cecil Rhodes). Mountains in other parts of the globe (Everest after British surveyor George Everest). Everest, not surprisingly, had many names before. Tibetan, Nepali, Chinese, Indian names. Names which meant things like 'Holy Mother' and 'Goddess of the Sky'. Do you see the change here? Whereby omnipotent feminine divinities are replaced by the name of a white bloke. Last year a group of local women made the first ascent of a mountain in Afghanistan (Berry, 2018). Together, they named it The Lion Daughters of Mir Samir Peak. *Lion Daughters*! It feels that could only have been named by them. Their contribution enriches the literature and the landscape.

The Decolonisation of Climbing

If you are climbing in an area which currently has no active, native climbing scene, when is it okay for you, as a British person, to name and claim all the key lines (and the minor lines) before that nascent climbing community has had time to develop? Imagine how you would feel as a local if, having gained climbing wherewithal, you find the rock surrounding your home purports to be labelled, route after route, by not-your-language names?

Maybe it's time to reconsider the belief, among western climbers, that rock lines are always free pickings. Perhaps it could become common practice to open in-depth communications with indigenous peoples before putting up new routes. What relationships currently exist with the rocks? What issues matter to various local inhabitants? Clearly, this would involve additional time, resources and money. It's easy to foresee problems with language barriers, cultural misunderstandings and consultation with nomadic populations, for instance. Nonetheless, isn't it worth considering taking climbing in this type of ethical, postcolonial direction? And the greater the power imbalance, surely the more effort should be made? However, to achieve this, we would need to prioritise sensitive listening over gung-ho adventuring and route-bagging. Can we self-regulate or should there be guidelines? Or would that mire our sport in bureaucracy?

What else, specifically, might ameliorate the colonising flavour of claiming and naming routes abroad? Money is frequently cited – that climbers bring cash to deprived areas, funding which is of significant benefit to local communities. Climbing is then like any other tourism. But can we do more? There must be many options, which may or may not seem familiar or viable at present. For example, is it possible to just climb and enjoy, without naming and claiming routes? Then this can be left to others, to locals, in due course. Is it different if you live there? If you are investing, long term, via language, friendships and finance, in the place you've made your home? How about supporting the development of a resident climbing community, sharing skills and kit? Or deferring on choice of route-names to indigenous peoples – why not leave marked-up topos with, say, the village elders, the school, the local women's co-operative, and ask them to name the lines? Names would then be in indigenous tongues and, translated into English, might provide insight into the locale as well as giving a sense of ownership to that community, in perpetuity.

The Perfect Line?

If 2003 was too early, is now the right time? Time to find a more perfect line when putting up new routes and giving them names. A perfect line in the rock face. A perfect line in the guidebook. A perfect line between climbing for yourself and respecting others. Between exploration and exploitation. Between past and present. Between what's lovely in theory but unfeasible in practice. Between doormat and collaborator and killjoy feminist. The perfect line when borders and genders and heart-body-mind are shown to be so fluid. The perfect persuasive or jarring sentence to trigger a debate.

Privilege:
Come Along for the Ride

Let us go on a journey. I'm choosing horseback. A friendly pace, with some degree of height, to get a nice view over some of the hedges. Plus you can pack a rack on a spare pony. We'll look at the open road, some jumps and the bumpety-bump of travel as a climber.

When the going's smooth? Just paradise. You and your steed in a picture-perfect lakeside camp! The clip-clop of a stony track! Galloping over the steppe! These are the times when you wake at South Stack in North Wales, slide open the van door to warm air and a stunning view, cliffs hidden beneath you and the lighthouse gleaming. Or topping out from a long, granite multi-pitch in Norway, at midnight, to watch the never-setting sun turn the sky wild, flamboyant colours. Or sand between your toes on a Thai beach, belaying your partner up a tangle of tree roots and preposterous tufas.

What a joy. Travel to gorgeous spots is one of the happy bonuses of climbing. Crags are frequently in beautiful, wild and unspoilt locations: sea cliffs, moorland outcrops, pinnacles and mountains. Personally, this sport has taken me globetrotting to California, the Arctic Circle, the Outer

Hebrides and beyond. To date, trips have been dictated by desire. One trip after another, to wherever I wanted – limited only by personal time and money. Riding roughshod! Lately, other factors are coming into play concerning environmental and cultural impact. In addition, due to age and changing circumstances, my travel preferences and methods have started to shift.

Putting the cart before the horse, let's start with that shift. As I get older I'm feeling the need to travel more slowly. I used to regularly fly out on climbing trips for a week or long weekend, climb relentlessly, no rest days, knacker myself out and come back exhausted. These days, short flights hustle my soul. Jet lag batters me. The abrupt flip of temperature, smell, different stars in the sky – too much! It doesn't feel right. It's not that I have less energy. I'm up at six in the morning, gallop up and down flights of stairs, go running in the hills. So it's not that I am getting tired, with age. It's something else.

When I first read Bruce Chatwin's *The Songlines* it was like looking over the stable door for the first time, and seeing open pasture. I was in my late teens and remember it keenly. It birthed in me the idea that there is a tempo at which we can comfortably move – and that is walking pace. Quicker than that is jangling, jarring. The book came out in 1987, before the technological era, before the Internet, before email, smart phones, Twitter and Instagram – so western life is a good deal more crammed and frenetic now. The point is, if we took a human baby from Australia or China or Nigeria or wherever, some X-thousand years ago, and brought that child up now it would have the same genetics, the same capacity for coping with modern life as a baby from the present. Which is to say – we have not evolved for this. I have not evolved to manage the speed of twenty-first century existence.

Accordingly, in these times, I am slowing down, restricting input, so I don't get overwhelmed. Potter gently in the van and go to local crags. Take fewer, longer journeys in preference to zipping hither and thither. Choose to move overland, on the surface of the earth, linking destinations, smelling the air change, watching the landscape alter, transitioning inside at pace with the view. Going slow – less to save the planet, than to save myself.

Which harnesses us up nicely with environmental impact – the first obstacle on the track. It's now commonly accepted that we should burn less fossil fuel. We all know why. It's bad for the earth's temperature and pollutes the atmosphere. We should cut down on flights. Thoughtless car-driving is frowned upon. Alternatives present themselves: electric vehicles, car-shares and car-pools; using public transport – the bumbling rhythm of a train or a country bus; going by bike or on foot – challenging with a rack, but not impossible.

Which takes us down the bridlepath of travelling light. Physically, having less stuff leads to a softer footfall, lesser transport requirements and a gentler hit on the environment. Climbing has been rather progressive in this regard over the past decade or so. Facets of the sport have revelled in becoming unencumbered, in casting off weight. Bouldering is increasingly popular (though the mats are enormous! Take a tip from old-style Bleausards who go bloc-to-bloc with nothing but the odd rag, tucked into a pocket). Deep Water Soloing made a huge splash. And in 2019 Alex Honnold upped the ante with *Free Solo* – no ropes, no gear, no partner and no water to cushion a fall. Soloing is travelling light. Soloing thins a rack right down. I have a friend who doesn't own many possessions, doesn't own a house, works odd jobs, travels around on his motorbike, stopping off at crags all over the world soloing long routes. Bravo!

Travelling slow and travelling light embody, symbolically, a draw towards the nomadic. Moving away from standard markers of success – career, income, status. Concentrating on the intangible – relationships, landscape, experiences, feelings.

I find myself compromised – I own a diesel van and often drive alone. Truck around with my bodyweight in trad gear and numerous different ropes for leading, sport climbing, abseiling and towing the van if ever, God forbid, I break down. So I am not an eco-warrior. But at the same time, don't wish to be an utterly unreformed gas-guzzler. How to negotiate this quandary, these hurdles, make my relation-ship with the natural world more promising – while still doing what I love?

Perhaps it's useful to view our life-choices more in the round rather than a single-issue hoo-ha about flight-shaming. Do we recycle, wear worn-out clothes, choose sustainable food? How about off-setting wider lifestyle decisions – do we volunteer with refugees? Check in on a neighbour twice a week? Pick up litter at the crag? Are we interested in reducing our carbon hoofprint and making a social contribution?

The way climbers engage in the environment – outdoorsiness, sea, sky and mountains – means we are, in my experience, overwhelmingly considerate of the natural world. As a community, we are well-versed in the Country Code. Beyond politeness, the peculiar tender-grappling intimacy of climbing truly lends itself to love. A kind of intimacy that bonds us across the Cartesian nature/culture divide. A flake of skin and a flake of limestone. Look at them mingle! This – if you want to go there – is radical, experiential, conceptual travel.

The second big jump is cultural impact. As a western climber, it is my responsibility to understand the context of my voyaging abroad. To understand that 'travel' is privileged – exploring, widening one's horizons, having a holiday all require time and/or cash and/or visas and passports. Less fortunate people tend to migrate, move across borders because of war or hunger. So *travel* is a luxury. Travel is generally what climbers do.

What were your inspirations to travel? I just cited Chatwin

– but these days I have reservations about referencing the culture and beliefs of aboriginal folks filtered through the pen of a white Englishman. Chatwin had an impact on me, way back, when I had neither awareness nor access to first-hand accounts. And, irrespective of his demographics, he was still a bona fide wandering soul! When chatting on this topic, a friend immediately mentioned Indiana Jones. Exploration! Daring! Good looks! Another cited Mr Benn, a children's cartoon starring an ordinary-looking, be-suited everyman who, each episode, would visit a fancy-dress parlour. Having chosen an outfit, when he changed his hat, he was transported to a different time and place, and the story began. It is notable that all these role-models of exploration are white guys, often with a taste for orientalism. Are our expectations of travel similarly slanted, albeit subliminally – that we deserve an experience, that the 'foreign' territory is primarily there as a setting for our amazing adventures?

Contrary to the adage, it's timely, as westerners, to look our advantages in the mouth and study the back teeth of our blessings. Having awareness of colonial history and ongoing power imbalances is surely de rigueur for any low-impact trip. In British climbing culture, am I right in thinking self-knowledge and cultural sensitivity are still regarded as secondary add-ons rather than central requirements? Do we need to re-appraise some of our assumptions, our habits? If we're on horseback, we surely have to wonder whether we should be sitting on a horse at all. Has the horse consented to this? Did it want to be broken? What are the dynamics? And here they are – the uncomfortable questions, the potential losses. Just because I love horse-riding, does that mean it's ethically justifiable to ride? Just because I adore galloping to crags in remote – through western eyes – parts of the world, when is it okay to go clambering up them?

What about our appearance overseas? Climbing clothing – short shorts and skimpy bra-tops – when is that okay, and when is it disrespectful? Do we even know when we perform actions that are disrespectful? Pointing our feet at someone in Indonesia, for example, is offensive. Plonking our dirty climbing shoes on the table or bar – do we realise the eyebrows we raise?

There are sacred rocks all over the globe. As Brits, do we let people boulder on Stonehenge? No, we don't. Locals in other countries and cultures might want money, or a prayer, or you to keep off their rock faces altogether. Will you respect this? Or nip in and nip out, and hope no one spots you cantering off? A courteous thoroughbred or a stubborn mule?

I find myself something of a donkey. Lugging about that big cross on my back. I try to be good – but no doubt I love exoticism as much as the next white person. I've climbed desert towers without contemplating their spiritual significance. I have photos I took in the early 1990s of Rajasthani women cowering behind their headscarves – pictures I now see as horribly intrusive. So I have no place on a high horse. I'm just trying to open up a thought process, rather than let colonialist behaviour go unchallenged. That is to say, come with me to the trough…

By the way, in my home country, I have a powerful sense of entitlement – I do want access to cliffs. Commonly, around me, it's private landowners or the military who are preventing or limiting such access. I understand the reasons given – issues of liability, concern for safety and/ or pure meanness (anyone remember Vixen Tor on Dartmoor?). But when it comes to religious objections, and the land isn't mine by any stretch – is it really my prerogative?

If we want to climb further afield, maybe a plan is to learn more and listen better. Make efforts to be aware of, and respect, indigenous peoples' opinions, stories and feelings. Is this viable? While I'm pretty sure the answer is 'yes', I am catholic as to methods. Conversations with locals have got to be a winner. Academic studies, perhaps. Or historical publications. My preference is via the arts: dance, paintings, music, novels and poetry. Get acquainted with throat singing in Mongolia! Study flamenco in Spain! One of the reasons I love arts as a mode of education is that they can lead to a visceral, not just intellectual, understanding of aspects of a country.

What we do as climbers, at our best, is boundary-crossing. Interacting with other peoples can build mutual understanding, respect, tolerance of difference. Bouldering in a mixed-nationality group, say, where we share the language of movement, laugh at the comedy, support each other's attempts and ascents – this is when climbing goes beyond divisions and facilitates powerful, corporeal integration. At these times, climbing is performing at the top of its game. The equines go gambolling over the plain, in a cloud of chalk dust.

I'm now going to amble on about van-life for a moment. Van-life is an evolving side-saddle. An ambiguous conundrum. On the one hand it burns diesel, which is terrible. On the other, it is a form of low-impact living. A van takes less electricity to run than a house, fewer raw materials to build. Living in cars and vans has long been a part of zero-rent climbing pragmatism. It makes sense! Transport to various crags and in-built accommodation. Sometimes the gathering of Transporters is like a Volkswagen convention or a mini-festival. My T4 is a lumbering, elderly shire horse of a vehicle. I delight in the freedom of van-life. To move or not to move, to stay or go, the fabulous views. Though it's a strange road – somewhere between feeling smug and being an object of pity, depending on who you're talking to.

Non-climbers accost me, fairly regularly, with phrases along the lines of 'You're so lucky, gadding about'. This is true. I am lucky. But, when these are other middle-class westerners, I don't think this is what they mean. When people say this phrase, what I hear is *I like what you're doing, but not enough to make the choices you've made.* They have prioritised their nice clothes, their job status, their reliable income, their steady relationship, their stylish house. Dirtbag life isn't really for them.

One interesting, detrimental, consequence of van-living is how it can slip into silo-mentality. You don't meet people on public transport, or in restaurants, or in hostels – as all these functions are self-contained in your metal box. I am guilty of this, for sure. Weeks on the road without interacting with anyone other than my climbing partner, and the odd supermarket cashier. So then it's good to have coffee in the community cafe or a trip to the pub after climbing – to meet other people, and put some money into the local economy.

For the past two decades, climbing trips have framed and defined my expenditure, my timetable and my identity. Travel is my default recourse when I'm confused and don't know what else to do. Travel shakes everything around, like when your mount bolts off unexpectedly. Everyday experiences are heightened and made visible. Buying food. Getting warm. Going from A to B. Gone is the complacency of habit! Everything is new, more challenging, requiring thought. A parallel shake-down happens internally – I get to re-appraise what is important to me, where I'm at in my life, what I am doing on the planet. Who I meet, the places I find, moments of serendipity attain a special significance. Bad things happen when I stay in one place too long. I lose confidence. Forget who I am. Even when I'm injured, or without a climbing partner, I'll wend my way along a steeplechase of climbing destinations.

Because I know I'll be able to park up there and be among compatriots, can talk their language, know enough of their code to fit in. A home from home, anywhere on the globe.

As travelling climbers, we derive an enormous amount of joy from getting on physical material (a boulder, a skyscraper, a mile-high vertical cliff), and moving about on it, with it. We do this in different locations, with different motivations, meeting different people. Horses for courses, as they say. None of it is innocent, for travel is an ethical decision as well as being hedonistic. An internal journey as well as the physical trek. A sacrifice of resources in return for non-guaranteed, unpredictable gifts.

Well. That was the ride. So far. Or just a few places, anyway. My hobby horse is flagging now, so we're going to make camp here and watch the stars for a while.

EXHAUSTION

Exhaustion:
The Big-up

Back at the hut, he gets a chopping board and one of the frying pans and lays out the vegetables and begins to peel and slice an onion. Let's call him Geoff. Another, slightly younger man is there, also beginning to cook. The younger man asks pleasantly what we did today and Geoff recounts our expedition up the three-star E2 which, despite its stars, clearly isn't done very often because the path to it over bracken and gorse was barely beaten-down and the crack was full of dust. Geoff reports that it is a top quality line and rates it as highly recommended. Geoff doesn't say he hung repeatedly, dropped a wire in the sea and used the abseil rope to dog the crux.

There is a cultural expectation on men to over-perform. This is very tiring.

Dislocation:
Cyborg-climbers –
Come to Your Senses!

Are we losing touch with our senses? Mina Leslie-Wujastyk, a world-class climber, has recently written about her diagnosis of Relative Energy Deficiency in Sport. She described her progressive dissociation from hunger, from tiredness – how she mentally pushed through physical warnings, controls and barriers. Looking around, such disjunction from the body appears increasingly fashionable in this hobby of ours. But our sport is so visceral! So tactile! What's going on?

Over the past twenty years I have borne witness to the professionalisation and commercialisation of rock climbing. Partly this has been fabulous, and led to more opportunities and wider access. On the flip side, aspects of this apparent progress are problematic. In this chapter I explore some questionable developments in training and nutrition, where climbers are following regimes rather than listening to their bodies. This is a cultural change and, as such, it seems to me that Leslie-Wujastyk's experience did not happen in isolation. Even non-professionals can find themselves alienated from how they feel and what they need.

Hunger Is Your Friend

Let's look at food. There are two devils emerging here. One is under-eating and the other is quashing of flavour. More has been written elsewhere on the perils of calorie-counting and dieting which reduce food to numbers and statistics. Here I am going to focus on the brutalisation of taste.

Food used to taste great. Soup, flapjacks, beans on toast, banana porridge. Increasingly I see meals being reduced to nutritional food groups. This is always a red flag for me. When something which tastes nice (i.e. food) is separated out into component parts which can be sold for profit, my alarm bells ring. There is talk of 'fuelling' rather than eating. Like a car.

A current fad in my immediate community is protein. My housemates all have protein powders. The drying rack is always stacked with cross-hatched protein shakers. Does this raw protein really improve people's performance? Whatever food fads have passed me by in the last two decades, don't climbers continue to function broadly similarly? It seems a case of Emperor's New Clothes – as each new marketed product comes out, everyone reinforces each other's faith in its efficacy, so they don't seem a fool. Wouldn't it be better (or just as good, and cheaper) to eat a balanced diet of delicious food? And even if these protein waters and electrolyte chewing gums and vitamin bars etc actually do work, do increase function by X per cent, do make us bigger and stronger and more fabulous than we are as normal human beings – what are the implications? There has been a shift from doing activities because we love them, to doing exercise because we want to look and perform like world-class athletes, like machines. We've become cyborg-climbers.

Crucially, all my housemates turn the unhappy ends of their sad mouths down and say how terrible the shakes taste. Tricks to disguise protein powder are exchanged. Whizzed up in smoothies with other (real) food. Sprinkled (just enough to give a decent protein dose, not so much as to kill the meal) on top of anything from stews to cereal. What has been sacrificed? The taste buds. The delicious, tender, loving buds which like to savour blackberries and roast lamb and almonds, damp and fresh, from the shell. Separated-out protein tastes so vile that surely it teaches the taste buds to numb themselves, out of self-protection. And when taste becomes numbed, they can sell you anything.

How alienated are we? One observation is on the weaponisation of food. Have you noticed snacks with brandnames like 'BODYARMOR' and 'Grenade'? Look at the packaging. Who is this for? It is gendered in a way which reinforces toxic masculinity – black/grey with unsparing, war-like fonts. Is this food? Or ammunition?

What is actually in these products? They appear to be, fundamentally, sugary drinks and confectionery with caffeine and extras. Squash, really. And candy bars. Being marketed like military hardware. Do we really want to eat some body armour, a grenade, a few bullets and swallow a sword?

Even at the softer end, innocuous bottles for water have phrases like 'Adventurecapitalist' emblazoned on the side. A protein shaker promising to 'Fuel your ambition'. Wow. What's wrong with 'Enjoy the taste!' or 'Thanks for using a re-useable container, thus reducing plastic waste' (not snappy enough?). As it is, the slogans advocate one-up-man(sic)-ship through a beverage. World domination through a drink.

What is going on with these products? They do not accord with the men I know, the climbers I know. Climbers have always been non-conformist, environmentalist, welcoming to outsiders and outliers, sensitive in unexpected ways. Haven't they?

We are being encouraged to eat like soldiers, like astronauts. A food pill. A dose of white powder. An injection of winning-formula. Where's the flavour, the subtlety, the joy of different textures? The juice of an apple, crisp-snappy? The butter-melt in a baked potato?

By a trick of marketing, we are beginning to lose touch with our internal signals of hunger and taste.

Tiredness Is Your Helpmeet

Over-exercise is another dysmorphia in our sport. Mina Leslie-Wujastyk did not rest her body sufficiently. She kept going and kept going and didn't listen to her flesh.

She's not alone. Another remarkably successful fad in the last twenty years has been training. We're all training now! But it wasn't always so. When I started climbing, no-one used to train – they just climbed. We went to Pembroke and Fontainebleau and multi-pitch crags in Spain and no-one trained. To clarify, I am not keen on going back to 'the good old days'. Way more alcohol was consumed, for a start, and pretty much everyone smoked. So there were problems then too! Just different ones…

By 'training' I mean doing peripheral activities spoken about as support activities to climbing. Like finger-board-ing, TRX, core sessions, conditioning, beast-makers, circuits, campusing… The tone is different – numerically based and less driven by spontaneous desire. Leisure has become job-like with schedules, measurements and performance targets. Again, a machine-like quality, more cyborg than human.

How effective is it? Greater strength can be a godsend and really boost confidence – all good! But without a well-in-tegrated programme, there can be gaps between training and performance. At its worst, repetitive training of one intense action primarily makes us better at that specific, dissociated movement. How transferable is it outdoors

– will it help you on real rock, any more than if you'd spent that time doing more actual climbing? Indeed, hasn't training indoors cut into time that could have been spent in nature, on our wild and lovely cliffs and crags? Has it become obsessive, an end in itself? How long-lasting is the gain – doesn't it disappear if you take time off? Wouldn't your focus be better spent improving your technique? Why has training become so ubiquitous?

Has it been promoted in a consumer culture because training can be lucrative? Sales of equipment must have soared in recent years. An industry of talks and work-shops, online and offline courses and regimes. No one used to sell us anything, when we sat at the crag. I am not against training per se. I am too permissive for that. But I am interested in the shift, the expansion of training as a phenomenon. Because if it was a beautiful, healthy, utopian world, would we climb? Of course. Would we train? Well…

The problem with training is that there is precious little credence given to how you feel, whether you feel tired, whether you have done enough for today. No. You have another hundred reps to do on your schedule, so the agenda is followed, rather than the needs of your body.

This cyborg-culture can be especially harmful to young climbers, some of whom are soaking up prevailing ideas on training, diet and weight loss. Climbing then becomes tied up with measurable performance, control and deprivation, rather than being a place of freedom, exploration and joy.

Why are these changes happening? No doubt there are a dozen explanations. I'm going to focus on two – the prioritisation of our visual register and the western notion of constant growth.

Prioritisation of the Visual
(= how you look matters more than how you feel)

From the first dozen years of climbing, I have very few photographs. Grainy bum-shots. Faded film-print. Nowadays, as we know, everyone (in the west, of a certain demographic, including most climbers) has a smartphone. We take digital pictures all the time. Rock climbing and bouldering photographs seem custom-made for the Internet age. Look at that muscle tone! Those guns! Those abs! Sometimes people seem more concerned with getting a good picture for social media than with the experience of climbing. Our virtual realities are very demanding.

In this context, it is important to be slender and fit and well-presented, constantly, as the camera could catch you at any moment. Instagram dictates we should be more toned, thinner, younger, more muscular. Hungry? Tired? No time for that! Chin up! Smile! How we look is gaining precedence over how we feel.

As a brief detour into clothing, it seems pertinent that

we used to wear our oldest, most broken clothes. Climbing involved getting smeared in mud, chalk and guano. Climbing involved snagging leggings on sharp, limestone jags; the abrasion of knees and seat by granite and grit. We would change out of everyday clothes into mismatched battered tops and holey long johns in the car parks. We would wear clothes we found at the roadside or in lost property bins. And then go to the sea cliffs and rubbishy quarries and get messy.

Little by little we learnt to stop wearing patched fleece trousers left over, unclaimed, from a house party, and learnt to spend £69.99 on some jeans with a climbing brand name.

I have some of these jeans, in fact. They are rather lovely. There's been an evolution of independent, ecology-conscious, non-sweatshop climbing-wear springing up like fairy toadstools in the present climate. I want to look like everyone else. I want to blend in. I want to support the small, local manufacturers. I like the new colours and the flexible fabrics. I'm a sucker too. I'm corruptible.

Which is to say, it never used to matter how we looked. And now it does. Even to me.

Constant Growth
(= we must always be getting better and better)

In western, consumerist, late-capitalist society we inhabit

the fallacy of constant growth. The rampaging impossibility of this philosophy has been exposed by environmentalists. Our planet lacks the resources to deliver never-ending expansion and so it has been necessary to challenge this orthodoxy. Extrapolated to our sport, why the constant expectation of bigger and better, faster and harder performance? How about sustainable climbing with fewer injuries, more work-life-play balance, more longevity?

In reality, I suspect bumbling along is how the majority of climbers, both old and young, actually climb. But how much is this world-view represented? Why does a VS climber apologise for being a VS climber? Why should someone on juggy resin swirls feel embarrassed about being on juggy resin swirls? Why is this not acceptable, worthy, enough? As if pottering about is some kind of moral turpitude. Why is enjoyment deemed lesser than ticking harder, higher grades?

Why do you climb? To punish yourself or for pleasure? Both are eminently possible, it is a sport for all proclivities. But if you climb for pleasure, where does happiness lie? In the appreciation of landscape, the pas de deux of movement, niceness of touch, companionship, tactile loveliness, that mental spaciousness, the full-body sigh where you get away from screens and desks and traffic jams and laundry and shopping lists and relationship complications and experience bliss. Can't you just do this, revel in this, be this?

Why 'get better' at all? Why 'improve'?

Someone Is Making Money

Do we need more supplements? To exercise more? Why? Who gains from this? We are being trained to concentrate on how we look and perform and, almost inevitably, that we don't look good enough or perform well enough. Products and services are springing up everywhere, ready to buy. Cosmetic surgery has gone up exponentially. Images of climbers are used to sell banking products and advertise business promotions. Someone is making money out of us.

Perhaps Neo-Liberal Late-Capitalist society is doing this on purpose, to divide us from ourselves and what feels good. The system is an animal, like any other, which wants to thrive and it does this best, and makes the most profit, by seeding anxiety and doubt and making you spend your cash. Most of all, you have to spend money. On protein powders and power drinks, conditioning equipment and training workshops.

Perhaps that's a little paranoid.

Let's say it's not a direct plan. Let's say I'm not talking a big conspiracy theory here, where the Powers That Be want me to forget the way it feels to brush my fingers over a slab of sunny granite – the way the rock gives out warmth like a huge, live bear; the way each crystal sticks, minutely, into the whorls of my tips. No. They don't care. De-prioritisation of our non-visual senses (taste, smell, whether we feel tired or hungry) is just collateral damage from the money machines. Our losses are merely a corollary, an unintended effect, unfortunate but inevitable. Like the way agricultural sprays led to the destruction of butterflies and bees. What a shame! They were just trying to get bigger and better crops!

Have That Giant Roast Dinner and Take a Nap

Do we need to come to our senses? Debate whether we have to be continually dieting, fasting, eating isolated food groups, counting reps, pulling up, wearing weight belts, drilling circuits, dead hangs, pushing ourselves? There is a dehumanising rigidity about this cyborg-climber culture: numerical over the sensual, procedural over the passionate. It is making some of us ill.

Feelings are an ecosystem. It's important we know when we're happy, sad, tired, lonely, energised, hungry, uncertain, relaxed. But we are not being trained how to feel. Do you feel good? Hurray. You win. Do you move like a ripple of water? Lord be praised. Do you eat when you're peckish and stop when you're full? Do you know when you're craving salad or a pork chop – and satisfy that? Do you know when you need to rest? Then lie down for a nap in the afternoon, or watch *Fleabag* and have an early night, rather than go to the gym. Responding to how we feel keeps us safe and healthy.

We need to consider what relationship we have with our bodies. Is our corporeality an inanimate tool, mechanism/ machine, slave, something *other*? Or a friend, a counsellor, an intimate, a guide, a companion with whom to have fun, an equal? Physicality as the *self*. Asking ourselves how it feels, how we feel inside, how the rock feels, seems good medicine in these times.

Repulsion:
Clearing the Space

The group of boys, young men, shirts off, strong, they're working this problem, they're working this mid-grade problem, maybe they're students or surveyors or legal executives or in retail, they're taking it in turns, watching each other, shouting suggestions, working the problem, the ones who aren't battling the plastic sit on the mats chatting, not meant to be sitting on the mats but everyone sits on the mats on a late Friday evening when it's quiet and they've made a camp of it here and they're chatting and taking it in turns and I drift by in my long white hair, picking out routes like fortune cookies and come to their problem, start gentle on the holds and the feel of them and punch up with my twisted feet and go-and-go-again and make the top flattie both hands soft as petals on a lake and slope down the wall like a cat taking the back way down by the garages and when I touch down all delicate step on the matting and turn it is empty, the young men are not there, the young men have all of a one-ness stood up, the young men have walked away without discussion, the men have gone elsewhere to another part of the wall to another problem, it was not clear they had finished with this problem but now they are no longer interested in it.

Attraction:
Revolution at Albarracín

It was a bright day and I was somewhere new. Circled about on my own. No boulder mat, no topo. Scrambling easy blocs. Orbiting. Getting to know the crag, the rocks, the space in between. Attracted by a large constellation of men and women – noisy, shouting, laughing – with multiple, giant pads. Span off. Floated untethered, disappearing and appearing, but always, somehow, drawn in by gravity to this big collective. Came across them again at a roof problem. High. Decent holds. I fancied this! No way I would try it unsupported. I am observed, a lone star, some kind of comet. Beckoned in. We smile. We are beaming. Spanish! English! Climbing is the language. Ushered to the mats, spotters below, a guy above, gesticulating. Step on and reach, arc upwards, lost in the din of the yelling and calling, all the planets, a whole solar system as I top out, slapping the sandstone, sticking it, surviving! And that was that. Spent the whole day together. Everyone half my age. In sync around the sunshine of the boulders.

POPULA-
THE

Expansiveness:
Setting the Style

Route setters are the wall gods. They stride around the matting with their Hilti and Makita drills and look divine – their whims translated into resin, a hallowed blend of intrigue and art. They are the omnipotent apex of indoor wall glory. They dictate the tone, the style, the techniques, the way. They control how we climb. And, where I live, they are almost all men.

Female setters are really needed, both to put up fantastic problems geared around women (more technique, more balance, more slabs, more twist, more fun, more comedy), and as role models. When a competition is running, for instance, how good would it be to see equal numbers of male and female setters?

Why are there so few female setters, and how can it be remedied? Which embedded hurdles prevent women from becoming eligible for training (exclusionary minimum climbing grade, recruitment within a closed circle of contacts, an assumption that women can't handle power tools?) or from flourishing in the role (lack of encouragement, an over-burden of expectation?)? What exactly is barring women from this super-cool job? Perhaps the message could go out to female staff, girls, women and the community that female setters will be trained, rewarded, appreciated and employed and that jobs are available and they will be welcomed – not in tokenism, but to provide a richer, more diverse range of setting possibilities.

Because style of set can get in a rut. Too reachy. Lack of footholds. Which clientele is being privileged? Whose feedback is really being listened to and acted upon? Do the 'hard boy' setters put up problems for their 'hard boy' friends? Is disproportionate attention channelled into upper echelon grades? Perhaps the same amount of time and resources and concentration should be spent on low and mid-grade routes as is typically focused on hard ones. Perhaps specialist setters (a fifty:fifty gender split?) could be employed, concentrating on these middling grades. What happens if this is done?

I appreciate that route setting is a tough profession, entailing hard physical labour, acid-washing, early mornings and late nights, long journeys, relentless imagination. Nevertheless, the job has perks and carries influence. Given goddess status, I'm convinced women could achieve quite splendid feats, in between receiving burnt offerings of coffee and resting on those dense, foam clouds of matting.

Dynamism:
Suggested Approach for Competitions

Setting

1. Allocate an equal amount of wall space for women's problems and men's problems. Measure it.

2. Spend an equal amount of money on holds used for women's problems and men's problems. Count it.

3. Spend an equal amount of time setting and fore-running women's problems and men's problems. Time it.

4. Ensure a parity of move-styles for women's problems and men's problems. If one gender has crimps, gastons, jams, dynos, side pulls, heel hooks, no-hands teeter, pinches, slopers, an au cheval straddle and the other has a row of jugs – then re-set to make them equally interesting. Feel it.

5. Employ an equal number of male and female route setters. Sort it.

General

1. Equal prize money, of course.

2. Do not allow a man in trainers to flash the women's problems just before the start of the competition (or, indeed, just after it ends).

3. Encourage parity, top to bottom – competitors, audience, setters, belayers, judges, DJs, comperes. The 'Gender Flip Test' is useful – imagine the whole scenario with genders reversed – would anything stick out as remarkable?

4. Observe the audience. If they spend more time watching the men's final, say – consider how to redress this, in the future, through the setting, or the location of the problems, or the timing of their slots, etc so that equal time is spent watching, and supporting, the women and girls.

5. Talk with the audience. Generate feedback systems so everyone feels at liberty to contribute constructively – bearing in mind everyone usually wants to support the walls and the comps and doesn't want to kill the vibe.

WALL II

SURPRI-
THE

Biliousness:
Threads

'Unfortunately this one is garbage. I found myself disagreeing with the premise of almost every paragraph. It is also poorly written and so poorly structured that I stopped half way down.'

'Absolute horseshite. It's like someone's kid being indulged and let loose at their parent's work.'

'… this article and the recent piece of new age psycho-babble […] must be hot contenders for shit article of the year. Useless premise, badly formulated.'

'So I'll just say that this is some of the most moronic crap I've read on ukc.'

'What a truckload of tosh.'

'Personally i think we use the bra size scale as a new grading system.'

'[…] have we ever stopped to ask ourselves – why are

we bothering to read another Sarah Jane Dobson piece?'

'Sarah Jane Dobner is made up isn't she. Has anyone ever actually met her? This is like the climbing version of The Onion except it's absolutely shite.'

'Ah, so this is what happens when you robotically apply the formulas of identity politics to climbing. Totally predictable, in other words, with that strange combination of an utterly conformist message being wrapped up in a package of self-congratulatory 'radicalism'... [...] f*ck the internet and what identity politics has done to the minds of people under 25.'

'I haven't engaged with it because it isn't worth engaging with. We've all seen all these points made a hundred time before, just not applied (quite so directly) to climbing. There is nothing new here, it's just cheap application of a very boring and by now very well established political line - which for all its cries of being subjugated and powerless, is *in my world at least* (academia) totally hegemonic (to use a phrase this sort of stuff usually likes) and brooks no dissent. I have to put up with enough of this pseudo-intellectual group think repetition in my working life, so it's mildly irritating seeing the boring superficial plays being applied to my hobby.'

Alongside the biliousness are many helpful, funny, serious, critical, exploratory, reflective, engaged responses – the vast majority contributed by white guys.

Intermingling:
The Salty Dance Floor

Still from *The Salty Dance Floor*

Dobner & Gromen-Hayes, 2018

'I love it when people try to do something different. What made *The Salty Dance Floor* stand out for me was its attempt to express an emotion that I have felt as a climber, so in that respect it was a very pertinent film for me. And it used the medium of film to not try to explain or verbalise this feeling, but to put the feeling across. What was the film saying? I have no idea, but I understood it.'

Niall Grimes, BMC TV Women in Adventure Film Competition judge, 2018

Community:
In the Blood

This piece was written ten years ago. At a time when trad was Queen. When indoor walls were a substitute if it was wet or dark outside. When the gang was tight and death was round the corner. It's very different now. Climbing has opened up, walls are gyms and the vast majority of the clientele never touch real rock. Bouldering is King and young climbers seem friendlier, more group-orientated, more having-fun than having-epics. So a different flavour to the community. While this piece has a historical ring to it, my feeling is that we are still a family – just more diverse, more generous, more Millennial.

I'm trying to book a holiday. It's not as easy as it seems. Not now. It used to be simple; my climbing boyfriends and I would say 'Let's go to Pembroke/Swanage/Costa Blanca/ the south-west deserts of America!' and Baby Bull would pack some clothes and twenty children's books and we'd set off and that was that. For a decade. It worked! The holidays were amazing.

But now I inhabit a world of conflict and juggling. Of grief. I suggest, 'Let's go here! And do a teeny-tiny spot of easy climbing!' And Bass String, a non-climber, says, 'Climbing?

Climbing?! You don't even do climbing any more! Let's cycle to Hamburg festival and watch Chilly Gonzales.' And Baby Bull says, 'I don't want to go. You two go. I'd prefer to stay at home.' And in the end we don't really go anywhere except occasionally, in an act of desperation, I drive myself to Pembroke just to get out of town and look at the sea. But two days on my own in the van isn't really what I'd call a holiday. And leisure-based vacations, without climbing, still seemed awfully hollow somehow.

There are issues with trad as a pleasant family amusement. By contrast, whole families can be Arsenal fans. Do board games together. Have sailing in the blood. But old school climbers are different. They function with an individual, burning, anti-social passion. An E3 lead isn't a jolly Sunday outing with the kids. It's something where you might die. Or break a leg, bust your heels, give yourself head injuries. How many people spell out to their parents the risk they've just taken on a sea cliff? In detail?

Adventure climbing is the antithesis of a conventional shared activity and as such is a refuge for the oddballs, a magnet for rescue cases. Assemble here the ones who can't relate fully to their families because it's not enough! Make room for those who can't sit in the pub and watch the Premier League because it's not enough! Come, the ones who got kicked out of school and threw in work because it's not enough! Gather round at the crag. And a new family is born. I love that family. It felt like the first family where I'd truly belonged.

Off to Portland at 6.30am on the weekend; staying in the Peaks in a camper van in January; getting off Baggy Point at 11pm on a June night to find the pub still open; these were the glory days: epic, luminous, driven. But it's a harsh clan. A caribou herd that gallops and gallops its exhilarating way but if you drop out through a snapped tendon or a bad knee the herd will leave you behind. They're too busy driving to Dinas Cromlech. Or Stanage Edge. So when I dropped out of climbing, with injury and a boyfriend who was more interested in music than rocks, I assumed I'd be eaten by wolves in the abandoned snowy wastes of the tundra.

But you know what? Something else happened. Something kinder and richer and more complex. As the main herd galloped away, I kept a hardcore of life-long super-close kin. Plus on each migration, the passing herd always remembered me and showed me I was welcome, if I fancied tagging along. More than this, I found the wolves largely left me alone. The Climbing Family had taught me a lot. Taught me how to be myself, however awkward and unacceptable that might be. Taught me to be brave and do what I needed to do. Taught me that I need not disintegrate in a room full of people because, behold, I'd led X-rated routes in Avon Gorge and survived and that magnificence stays in your heart, firm and quiet and you don't need to say anything to anyone about it. I'd changed. I was able to function much better in the Outside World than I'd done before being a climber. Indeed, these days I can watch both halves of an Arsenal match, play Monopoly without swishing the tiny houses and hotels on the carpet, sit in a boat and watch the horizon for hours. Almost have holidays like other people do.

Do I not climb any more? It doesn't matter whether I touch rock or not. I looked up from my computer screen. Relax! Confused about booking a family holiday? That's a first world problem right there. I wasn't going to die of it! Everything was fine! Because everything is fine, if you put it in perspective with a bold trad lead. I left the easyJet site and shut the lid of my laptop.

As it happened, that evening was the annual climbers' party, a grand gathering of the tribe. I went along. Knew almost everyone. Stood at the bar with Dyno Monster, where we caught up with the community's gossip and misadventures, relived past triumphs and disasters and chuckled about the rescue cases, ourselves included. Looking around we could see the Young Ones coming through, the next generation of misfits.

Welcome to the Family, kids.

Thrill:
All the Creatures

We share the crags, we share the cliffs, we share the walk-
ins. We are entangled in every possible space with other
life-forms. Oftentimes it's clandestine and the birds and
animals hide from us but when there's an open meeting I'm
struck by the thrill, the humility, the interaction, the reveal.
Climbing is a good way to meet creatures. Something to do
with remote spots and slowness, the standing at belay, the
looking and being and the silence of humans. Hence the
seals who pop up and watch from the coast; brown bears at
Yosemite criss-crossing the path; lizards in Spain, skittering
vertically showing how it's done; a grass snake at the top
of St Govan's and gannets in the distance and choughs; the
mice at Fly Wall amongst alpine strawberries; the robin
who eats cake from your hand at Wyndcliff; a tarantula
at Joshua Tree; mating starfish at Lydstep; a blenny on the
belay at Mowing Word mouthing tips for survival at height;
dolphins slicing past South Stack; the jackdaw on Explod-
ing Galaxy Wall who dive-bombed me before perching a
metre or two away and tilting his head; the fox at Santa
Ana and a vomiting fulmar on the collapsing Culm. Other
climbers have stories of nests of bees and owls and basking
sharks and scorpions.

Connectivity:
Sea Cliff Bird Life

Herring Gull: Ninety-nine

The gull eyed me from the fence
Stood there in her pink feet
99 flake legs
Ending in strawberry melt

Looking for a cornet?
Turned her head this way and that
To see if I would drop
Wafer flakes and having no luck

Hopped down into the lot
As it was emptying out of cars
To peck up the pickings
Of a September Sunday tourist spot

Took her time and walked
From grassy plot to grassy plot
Methodically as far as the tarmac
Where the ice-cream van had parked

Chough: Red-handed

You! Corvid with extremities
Dunked in blood
Black cat with a red tongue
Lucky for most, unlucky for some

Born to be an emblem
Red and black poster-crow, yet
What lies at your heart?
Upright citizen or something darker

Protected now. Could preen willy-nilly
Why so shifty?
Black cloak, avoiding eye contact
As if caught red-handed. Whipping

Over the cliff. Black-and-red flit
Canny switch from bandit to mascot
Have you pulled a fast one?
Sword of your beak still wet

Gannets: Crusaders

A crusade of
Other-worldly birds
In the shape of the cross

White as righteousness
Heads dipped in gold
Kingly, way up the hierarchy

Only answering to God
And the call of shoals
Of knife-blade fish

Gannets fall like martyrs
And rise again
Swallowing sinners whole

Cormorant: The Hanged Man

Forever banished
Loitering on the blasted outskirts
Of coastal fringes and urban watercourses

Rehearsing over and over again
Being hitched to a gibbet and left to rot
A life of shame in

Second-hand clothing from the charity shop
Boots without laces
That tattered smock

So long ago now he's forgotten the crime
Aware only that society expects such remorse
From the hanged man

Fulmar: Foul-mouthed

Fulmars out-gull the gulls
Whatever associations come with the word *common*
Fulmars up the ante with their
Grey feathers, stubby wingspan, their thuggery

Tough motherfuckers, foul mouthed
Fish-oil vomit in a scrap. Next level!
Stuff the Queensberry Rules when it comes
To family and community. Fight dirty

Eggs on bare rock, scorn of mollycoddling
Old fashioned, brutal, loyal, brave
Their love uncommon. Spend their days at street-level
In the salt-air and spray of the waves

Belonging:
Landscape

I.

Rock climbing is tied in with globally beautiful locations. Yosemite valley. Desert Towers in Utah. British sea cliffs – Pembroke, Gogarth, the Outer Hebridean islands. The landscape becomes an extra companion. One who can keep you company if your climbing partner cancels at the last minute because they've twisted their ankle or missed the train.

II.

The rock, whether limestone or sandstone or granite or slate or gneiss or conglomerate doesn't appear to be concerned whether you are female, non-binary, male, gay, straight, Black, white, of colour, an amputee, blind, deaf, poor or wealthy, middle class or working class, fashionably dressed or in rags and in that way is indiscriminate.

III.

As I get older, landscape becomes paramount in my climbing life. I am slightly fussed by grades, yes. But I would choose, every time, a fabulous Hard Severe in an amazing position on a gorgeous sea cliff or a high mountain pass rather than a nondescript E2 in a quarry. The view matters to me now. It strikes me this is something to do with age. I recall being a child and looking out of the car window and feeling no connection at all with the faded hills. I remember my own daughter, as a three-year-old, not being able to focus on a rainbow – it was too far away. Nowadays my years are linking me to that distant landscape. I belong in the panorama. Not in an important way. I belong in the way a blade of grass belongs. And this belonging is a gift because, for a long time, I didn't belong anywhere.

IV.

I am seven. I live in fields. I have no friends. I hang out with two ponies in a little stone shelter. I know where the one maroon primrose is, amongst the yellow flowers. I sit inside the bare branches of the laurel tree, where I have climbed. These are my places. This is safety.

V.

The cliffs at St Govan's, Pembroke – where my ashes will blow onto ledges and drift into the sea. Burnt carbon, the dust of limestone. Not so very different.

Spirituality:
Living Rock

'After all, we do not know what it is like to be a rock because we are only human. The most we can do is project our minds into the rock so as to try and imagine the feelings experienced by a rock. For surely there is no reason why a rock cannot have a mind of its own. Though not of the human kind, nevertheless a feeling, a sensitivity to its surroundings.'

I. Thomas, 1967

How sensitive are we to our surroundings?

There are times when levering rocks off with crowbars doesn't feel right. When slapping on names seems an imposition. When my body responds with a weird kind of churning, a mild but insistent gut-level nausea. Where the prayer flags and incense, incantations and ceremony? Shouldn't we ask permission, give libation, sit for a moment with the crag, the gouged-out quarry, the de-ivied outcrop, the remote desert line, the imposing Alaskan rock face, and get on the same wavelength? What are the terms, what's sufficiently respectful, what price do we need to pay?

The rock is what it is. We don't own it. We live with it.

Many of us love it for its touch and its colours and its sweep and the sense of place it gives to a landscape, the way it pins the meadows and moors and sea to the earth. Mostly the rock is kind, and lets us climb. Other times it is loose, capricious, fatal, cruel. We routinely treat the rock like a passive, dead, inanimate resource which can be exploited and divvied up. But what if the rock is alive, sensitive, vibrant? Maybe it trembles when you approach with glue and a drill. Perhaps it has its own name.

Is that a step too far? Have I lost you? But these are post-human times, an era to de-centre the narrow perspective of Homo sapiens. As Anglo, western science moves on, and we discover that trees and fungi communicate in ways deemed impossible a generation ago, isn't it conceivable that what we currently consider insentient matter responds to its environment?

In addition to its own soul, rock has traditionally nurtured and accommodated the spirits of others. All over the world, crags appear to absorb and hold and house departed family, spirit animals, gods and goddesses: in North America, the sacred mountains of the Navajo; in Australia, Uluru for the Anangu; in Asia, Mongolian locals advising that their ancestors are in the outcrop.

These are not currently mainstream beliefs in the UK. Nonetheless, out of all of us in the west, perhaps climbers are most attuned to the vital and sacred nature of rocks.

Comedy:
Trickster

Buzzer

The rock asks questions
Tests you
Makes practical jokes
Invites your rejoinder then giggles when you fluster

A game-show host
Some kind of quiz-master
With a wicked
Sense of humour

You move, gripped
Hyper-conscious of the buzzer
Use sinew and muscle to fashion your answer
With some attempt at wit

Cabbage

Did you see that sling?
Looped over a barely-perceivable
Nobble
And the way I was chuckling?

Or the simple, loving joy
Of a perfect nut-slot
With a perfect nut-fit
Which makes you smile

Threaded wires! Or that useless cluster
Of RPs! Just silly
Much sillier than sport or bouldering
I imagine ice-climbing is droller still

The catch!
When you fell and were saved
As your rope wrapped around a cabbage plant
And it held

You know he bailed the pitch?
Lowered from his nut key hooked over a crystal
Then flicked it off
I'm sure the crag thought that was slapstick

The daftness
Of back-and-footing or jamming
Where you aren't actually holding on
To anything

Ribald, surely
With your helmet wedged
In a chimney
And you can't go up and you can't go down

Or lying horizontal
On a ledge smeared in guano
With a gull hawking
Fish-bile into your face

Whilst you blindly fumble
With your oily fingers
For any kind of grip
Could you choose a voluntary pastime more ridiculous?

The ludicrousness
Of how dangerous it is
You could die!
Somehow, hilarious

This dark, comic gut
Exposed when I was guiding
And someone looked at me as if I could guarantee their safety
Which spoilt all the fun

Humbled:
Zig-zag

Chattering on the walk-in, breakfast settling, the long drive here seeping away, not relevant, overlaid by careful steps up the stony path, puddles and streamlets hidden in bracken. I'm a visitor and this is the Ultimate Sanction's local crag. She walks ahead of me, sure-footed, the right kit, the right bag. I'm wearing one of her old coats, a cast-off. Follow in her tread. We hike our way up the first tier and when the path levels out, take a left and skirt the boulders beneath the higher escarpment. 'Look at that!' I call, excited by the grit, by the shapes, by the early morning and being out of the car and the grey musk of it all. 'That zig-zag crack looks amazing!' 'It's nasty.' 'No! It looks brilliant! Look at it! What's the grade?' 'Hard Severe.' 'Let's start here!' She doesn't say a word more. Barely raises an eyebrow. Keeps silent. There's a moment when we're both standing there, saying nothing. Then she firms her mouth in a very north-ern way and I tip off my rucksack and empty out the gear and she gets the ropes from her pack and begins to flake them on the cropped grass at the base of the crag. This is fun. I'm so happy. Playtime and my friend and the rock and a romping little starter, well below my grade. Rack up. Place one cam from the ground. Try and get established. Fret a bit. Stall. Step back down. Ask the Ultimate Sanction if she has any bigger pieces. She unhands the ropes – risk-free, as I'm standing right by her – reaches in her pack at a leisurely pace, holds out a hex. Places her hands back on the ropes, either side of the belay device. Her lips have not moved. In fact she is using minimal movement in her entire body. She is a statue. She has turned to stone. I turn to face the crag again, reach up on tippy-toes, fiddle with the chock, it should slot in! It doesn't, the crack's flared, the hex is tumbling out of my fingertips, it takes ages, it's not the best but it's stuck now half-in half-out, wedged, but badly, I'm out of breath, I haven't left the ground, maybe it's better higher up, perhaps I just need to get on it, get committed. Shove both hands in, scuffle with my left foot, grunt, wave my right leg around, try and wedge it sideways, fail, barn door, flounder, struggle on the jams, pedal my right leg in space again, flop downwards, ooze to the deck, heavy-breathing, my right knuckle bleeding slightly. Stand on my crumpled feet. Stare at the zig-zag crack. Hard Severe. Stand there some more. Rotate very slowly towards the Ultimate Sanction who, after one more stern pause, says briskly, 'Ready now?'

Companionship:
Pick and Mix

It's marvellous when I've just come back from the shops: chocolate eclairs, a box of blueberries, carrot sticks, fresh bread, Normandy brie, a carton of mango juice, Kettle Chips, Jaffa Cakes. I hate shopping with a passion, can't stand the jostling anxiety of choosing all those items, queueing to pay. But it's undoubtedly convenient and delightful, of course, when the cupboards are full and you can assemble a proper picnic.

If only you could go to the supermarket and purchase a climbing partner. 'Do you have any climbing partners?' 'Naturally Madam, would that be trad, sport or bouldering?' 'Wow! Er, trad mainly, though able to turn its hand to most things.' 'Would Madam prefer a male or a female?' 'Whatever's the most reasonable, thank you.' 'Disposables, Madam?' 'No, I'd like one for life.'

It's hard finding a good climbing partner. They need to desire the same kinds of route, want to visit the same places. In addition be at relatively the same grade, be competent, have compatible availability. You need to be happy spending all day with them on a car journey up to Scotland or in a pub at Land's End when the sea fog's taken hold. You need to trust them.

With a really fine partner your climbing can step up from a habitual pedestrian outing into something sublime where you rack up without words, spend an age on the crux without them blurting out, 'The tufa's behind you!', seconding's a joy and the ropes run like magic. You up your grade. You share sandwiches.

So what happened? How can I climb all these years and be struggling for a partner? Well. Many things happened, some to me, some to other people. First up? I mainly climbed with boyfriends. Which is splendid when it's going well: you share kit, transport, dreams, beds. But when it falls apart and you want solace on the rock, where is your climbing partner? You don't have one any more.

And what of the other folks? They do different stuff. They have lives. A top-slice of friends, for example, (Green Plastic Dinosaur! King of Kings!) began spending every winter out in Thailand. Climbing in the sunshine and being warm. I can't blame them. Then take White Rhino – consumed by childcare where once she would have been been up for a week-long trip every couple of months. I haven't managed a single weekend away with her for the past seven years. Two fabulous offspring, yes. All worth it. But still! Most gutting of all is the Ultimate Sanction who, after years of injury, recovered only to re-invent herself as a cyclist. Not any old cyclist either: she has the lycra, the medals, the regime, the team. Her house is full of *Procycling* magazines.

There are bikes in the bedroom, bikes in the bathroom. She's done it! She's found another fully satisfying activity! But where is she when I'm struggling to find a partner for Lundy?

On that point, holidays and even weekends away up the ante quite considerably. They involve overnight arrangements, they raise the gender issue. I never used to pay it any mind but a couple of things changed. Firstly I now have a non-climbing boyfriend. Bass String's a musician. If he announced he was going off with one other woman to an isolated spot for an intense piano workshop, let's face it, I wouldn't be too chuffed. So how is he going to feel about me heading off to a coastal crag with another bloke? The second thing was a recent incident at a pub in Cornwall. I've camped there many times and climbed with various partners at Bosigran, Sennen, Kenidjack, Gurnard's Head, St Loy, Chair Ladder and more. Whilst ordering dinner at the bar one of the locals lurched over and asked me if I'd have sex with him as I'd obviously slept with everyone else. Awkward. Could do without it. I just want to climb.

I am, of course, my own worst enemy. The older I get and the more I see, the more paranoid I get about who belays me. Being introverted I've avoided boisterous gatherings at sport crags. I appear to harbour a Disney-like fixation for The One-And-Only Prince/ess In Shining Armour trad partner and so have commonly declined invitations where I sense a chink of imperfection. And thus the pool has got smaller and smaller. Moody, opinionated, porcupine-like, scared, myopic and unforgiving, I hazard my character may have played a starring isolationist role. Some days I won't muster the effort to ask someone if they're free, lack the courage to send that text.

My New Year's Resolution was to buck up and get out there and sort more climbing. It's been nice. There's little momentum as I'm not, as yet, key to anyone else's ambitions. But I've been getting out with half a dozen different people and this has got me back on the rock. And that's what this is all about isn't it: the relationship with the rock. When it's all going well and you trust your belayer enough to forget about them, then you can switch your attention fully to the various skins of limestone, grit, granite; feel the warmth within; cajole the protection; slip into the bliss of ecstatic exposure; gaze into the savagery and tenderness of the rockface.

So then the climbing partner is a facilitator for a more all-encompassing relationship. The climbing partner is the dealer, the priest. It's not an insignificant role.

I haven't been shopping for a few days. So today's lunch is a pick-and-mix of leftovers garnered from all corners of the kitchen: a few squares of 85% chocolate, some out-of-date salami and a frozen malt loaf.

We'll see how we get on.

Trust:

Life in Your Hands

Partner

Climbing is used as a metaphor for trust
Their life in your hands
It is not a metaphor
Look hard at a new partner's
Attentiveness, their belay technique

Familiarity with crag etiquette
Will they save me
From the ground, that ledge
Will they encourage me
With voice and spirit and big-heartedness

Will they come with me
Up scree slopes, down gullies
In cold and heat, jumping across zawns
Abseiling into bays
With no obvious retreat?

Pulse

Few roles are as overt as a doctor
Regarding their power over mortality

By and large, we are heedless
Of the trust put in us. Become glib

Each time we give a passenger
A lift in our car, for instance

But when a rock climber
Moves away, delicately, up a cliff

Leaving the second in charge
Of the blue rope and red rope

They pulse, as if they really might be
The leader's vena cava and aorta

Tendril

Is it practice? Ten thousand hours
Of clasping, just so, on the quest
To be expert

Nursery ditty
Of *V to the knee, one-two-three*
Ingrained to the point of brainwashing

Muscle-memory
Of patterning the same dance
Over and over. A hand-jive. A tango

Even in sleep
Dreaming the sequence. A climber. A fall!
Wake with fists clenched

Instinct
This clawing of fingers. A reflex. Inevitable
As the green twirl of a pea-tendril

Tenderness:
Belaying as an Act of Love

A few months ago, I went on a training course to update my creaking SPA (Single Pitch Award) qualification in line with the sparkling new RCI (Rock Climbing Instructor). There were four of us attending, all dyed-in-the-wool trad climbers. Part of the syllabus dealt with safe belaying, at which point one of the delegates began making comments like 'Belaying! Isn't that when you switch off for an hour?' and 'That's when I usually read the guidebook!'

It seems to me there is a lot we never teach about belaying. It brings to mind school sex education in the 1970s – one lesson, basic diagrams, the physical mechanics. But no talk of love, care, the spiritual connection inherent in the activity. For belaying continues to get a bad rep. Gets pushed aside as the not-doing part of the game. A frustrating interlude before it's your turn to lead. The price you pay for someone else holding your ropes. At worst, simply wasted time.

It doesn't have to be so. Clearly there are occasions when it is cold and wet and uncomfortable belaying your partner. They're taking ages. You're on a hanging stance. They keep falling off and slamming you. Your neck aches from looking up. Yet it can also be beautiful – a place of care, of meditation, of appreciation.

When first introduced to climbing I was astounded at the responsibility of the belayer. It seemed phenomenal I was allowed to hold the ropes, and be in charge of the life or death of another human being, so explicitly. Because the whole purpose of the belayer is to keep the other climber alive. Which is done by managing a piece of string and a holey bit of metal. It didn't seem enough. Shouldn't there be a ritual, a blessing, some formal documentation to allow anything so extreme? But no. A few words. And their life in your hands.

It's very lovely to care for a creature and be accorded such trust. An honour.

The Second

Let's think about the ropes. Something magical happens. Each rope becomes a nerve, a single cell, stretched between the two of you. Feel it. Your top hand, resting on the nylon, fingertips alert, listening through your attentive, haptic, calloused skin. This is especially obvious when your leader is out of sight; has traversed a rib, stepped round an arête, climbed far above you and disappeared. Do you fish? Perhaps it's like this, handling the line, knowing weed from sand from pollack from bass. Knowing what is going on in the dark water.

You know the pattern. You know what happens, how climbing works. The pauses. A tricky section – was that in the description? More likely placing gear? Slide your grip a fraction down below the plate, ropes suspended in the merest Mona Lisa smile. Ready to hold a fall. Ready also, when a measured tug comes, to feed the rope through. The pull. You feed. Paid out a lot? An overhead runner. Visualise them bunging the wire from below, lumped by its own weight into the slot. You have them on this rope – take in slack as they move up. Simultaneously ease the other line out. You see this. You see it in your mind's eye. You know what is happening on the rock, out of sight, where your partner is climbing. You are following their progress with your hands and your imagination; keeping them as safe as you can with the tools that you have.

Some while later, coils at your feet subtracted from the pitch, you follow what is going on at the top. A long period of relative stillness? The fashioning of a belay out of multiple anchor points. A rapid pay-out? Swift walk to a pinnacle, or to stakes on a grassy rise. You know the land. You know when they're heading back to the cliff edge, ready to clove-hitch and equalise. You know.

All the same, you do not let go of the live end, or take off belay, until you are certain your leader is safe. Even if this means feeding the rest of the rope through the plate. That's just how it is.

By the time the leader has taken in all the slack and you've yelled 'That's me!' to the wind, you have your shoes on and all the gear out save one shiny staple or one bomber nut (assuming you're comfortable on a ledge, assuming that's reasonable having assessed the circumstances) and you're ready to second. This was how I was taught. The second services the leader; stands where they're asked, doesn't keep the leader waiting. An act of focus and attention. An act of tenderness. An act of love, for the leader is vulnerable and we need to care for each other.

That's when the leader takes care of you. Reeling in the enchanted, plaited strand of Rapunzel's synthetic hair.

The Leader

Sit. You're safe. You've survived. Breathe.

Breathe.

Now look. Look around. Look at it all. Look out and around at the wide, far view. Look as you've never looked before. Look and breathe. Look and breathe at the same time. Look around. What is here?

I recall watching the opening sequence of a film by Chantal Akerman. The extended, unedited shot, from a fixed camera point, is quite an average view, with quite an ordinary tree branch in the foreground. The colours are washed out, grey-grade, unremarkable. The branch blows a little in the breeze, from time to time. Nothing else happens. The more we look, the more there is to see. The branch, the view, the greyness, the everyday-ness. It becomes strangely hypnotic. An unwillingness to focus on anything else. Just this. Just this branch. Just this arbitrary view.

Something happens, belaying at the top of a climb. Specifically, at the top of a trad climb. It is one of the (many) reasons I'm especially fond of trad: a place for reflection, a time when the moment sinks in and I can just be. A space to be. To be me, here. In this landscape.

It's such a shock to be lowered straight down after a hard sport ascent. Where is my 'Forever Moment'? The stop. I remember when I gave birth to my daughter, on the sitting room floor of our rented flat, and the midwives grabbed her and shoved her straight on the nipple. I remember that. See the vocabulary: grabbed, shoved. That's not what anyone wants, is it? Pauses are good. Stops. Time to reflect. I would have preferred to come to, for a few seconds, and then gather her to the breast myself. To have control. To be calling the pace.

Belaying, especially at the top, is a natural opportunity for active meditation. The enforced sitting, combined with post-lead-I-didn't-die euphoria, lends itself to heightened awareness. My hands constantly feel the rope, testing and taking in or giving out, but mainly taking in. This happens pretty automatically now. It's body memory. It's what my hands will do. Which leaves my mind and heart free.

Look again. Observe the sun on the ocean, straight ahead, the shimmering, tripping road of light to the horizon; sea-surface utterly opaque, a choppy border between drenched and dry. When the sun's at your back, the water opens up and you're welcomed in. Can slide between waves, sense the surge of tides. See the starfish and kelp and bladderwrack. Look out for seals. A seal day is always a good day. They watch us and we watch them. I fancy they can read my features from all that way down in the briny swell.

From the top you can tell time by the rise and fall of estuary water. You can tell time by the height of the sun. You can tell time by how tired your forearms are; how exhausted your mind is from protracted fear. Can tell weather from the cloud banks; tell weather from the bird-song; tell weather from the yellow light which inevitably means time is up whether by inclemency (snow, storms) or nightfall heralded by the witching hour.

Look once more at the tiny things. Perhaps, while you belay, you will stare at this small fringe of lichen for an hour. Perhaps you will watch the play of wind over this grass-seed head, or this daisy. You might share the ledge with a woodlouse. Or ants. Or a baby gull. Do you feel the flood of love for the ants and the seal and the daisy and the ledge? This is your Forever Moment, or can be, no matter what a struggle the route has been. No matter you used your knees on that Hard Severe.

All this while, you are bringing your second up. Being sensitive to that traverse, to how tight they like the rope, making it a good experience for them. Something shared. Co-created. Mutually witnessed. Belaying ties us together physically, metaphorically and emotionally. With familiar partners, no one needs to speak about the process. They top out, we chat about the route, the conditions, the seals.

And while we do this, we're pulling the ropes through, retrieving gear, coiling in sync. Automatically and happily. It still fills me with delight, this tiny-team solicitude.

On occasions, when not climbing, I've taken myself to cliffs and sat down, alone, at the finishing stance of a familiar route. But the alchemy doesn't happen. Where is the glory, the specialness? It doesn't kick in for me without the lead. I am still reliant on the cocktail of self-made drugs – adrenaline, endorphins, dopamine, serotonin – to fully revel in the cliff-top polaroid vividness of living. But more than that, it doesn't trigger for me without a partner with whom to share the care and gratitude. And if I'm not tied in to a webbing of slings and nuts and cams, I get up and walk away without investing enough of my soul.

Maybe when I'm older, I'll be able to sit in the landscape and be, without climbing at all. Something to look forward to, perhaps.

OVERWHELMED

Overwhelmed:
Hammer and Feather

Here are some technical tips for a lightweight belay partner. Why? Because being smashed forwards and upwards into rock is painful and frightening and potentially dangerous.

It isn't all one way. For bouldering, heavier climbers have to trust to luck and be grateful their tinier partners have positioned the mat properly, and then got out of the way. By contrast, lighter-weight climbers can sometimes be caught and managed to the ground by their larger partners. This has definitely happened to me, and I am grateful. So it's not all moaning, see.

Many aspects of climbing are covered admirably elsewhere (Libby Peters' book *Rock Climbing: Essential Skills and Techniques* is the standard manual and I still carry it everywhere in the van). However, I don't often see guidance for taking care of lighter climbers, so that is what this section's about. If you're lightweight – love yourself! If your partner is lighter – show your love for them.

Weight discrepancy is often (but not always) gendered. You've seen the couples: a heavier male partner and a lower-mass woman. It also happens with, say, a parent being belayed by a child or youth.

An issue with this dynamic arises when the knowledge-base rests with the heavier partner. Quite often the parent has more knowledge than the child – the parent has been climbing for years, and now the child/youth is deemed old and big enough to belay them. The gendered classic is when more experienced, heavier men introduce their new girlfriends to climbing, and get the girlfriends to belay them. (I worked in climbing centres. I saw this happen many, many times. To be fair, I was introduced to climbing by a boyfriend who left me to belay for the first time, unaccompanied and unsupervised, while he headed up a terrifying chunk of grit. We both lived. Anyway. Moving on.)

So this happens all the time. The crux of the problem is that the heavier, more experienced partner often doesn't know what it's like to be a lightweight belayer. So they don't realise it's an issue and/or don't know the tips.

Here are some tips.

Positioning

Belaying from the ground, if your leader falls, you will be pulled towards the first clip, the first piece of gear. If you're lighter, you won't be able to hold your ground or provide a measured 'soft fall' – you'll just be whisked off your feet by the momentum. The place to stand is close enough under the first clip that the momentum hauls you upwards. Position your feet to manage your upward spring, and Bob's your uncle. If you stand or sit too far away from this first piece of gear, you won't go up, you'll go forwards. You'll go forwards quite fast and slam into the wall. This hurts, and you might drop your climber. Bad, bad, bad.

Learning is commonly the hard way. The tempter is usually a nice, rounded, comfortable rock about ten feet away. In the early days a girlfriend of mine sat on this nice rock, and when I fell off three quarters of the way up the route, she was yanked to the base of the climb, the bottom wires ripped from the outwards pull, and I was brushing the ground. We'd both thought the obvious 'belay rock' was fine when I'd set off. We were young. She was actually about the same weight as me. Things are just harder and faster and hurtier when your partner is larger.

As with much in climbing, use your imagination. If I stand here, what will happen to me when/if my partner falls?

Direct Belays

I'd been climbing for years before I knew about direct belays. I wish I'd known about them earlier. It's what instructors often do, and for good reason.

With direct belays, weight is transferred directly onto the tree, or the rock, or whatever you're belaying from. Not to you. This really comes into its own when you've led a climb, and you're bringing up a heavier climber, who then rests on the rope.

By way of illustration, years ago I spent many excruciating minutes/hours with my plate locked off, holding the weight of my twelve-and-a-half-stone boyfriend, with the rope slicing my thighs and the metal nose of the belay device digging horribly into my hip, while he painstakingly extracted stuck cams from various desert towers in Utah. In hindsight, I could have just chilled out comfortably and safely, having rigged a direct belay, hitching the rope up in guide mode.

I still have a couple of the cams, by the way.

Assisted Braking

Many belay devices on the market now have in-built assisted braking. Plates in guide mode offer assisted braking. Assisted braking is a particular boon when belaying a heavier partner, as you know even if you get jerked up horribly or battered on the head, you won't drop your climber.

Upward Pull and Close-by Roofs

Battered on the head? Yes, battered on the head.

If you're a lighter climber, and you're belaying below a nearby roof or overhang – red flag! What will happen if your leader falls? If *I will be wrenched upwards at lightning speed and my head and body lacerated on those dagger-like limestone projections* is the answer, try and do something to prevent this. Slinging yourself to the ground is a reasonable plan. Make sure there's no slack in the system so the rock absorbs the impact and you don't get jerked around. If you're on multi-pitch and just have two bolts in a cave feature, make a direct belay from those bolts and tie yourself in.

Clearly, I brained myself and embedded the ATC into my forearm when my fifteen-stone F6b leader found himself lost on an F7a and took a big fall. I had a helmet on, which was good news for both of us. But I was still injured. If I'd thought more about big-climber-little-climber-roof scenarios, and made provision, life would have been that bit better.

Also, none of these tips matters particularly if your heavier climbing partner doesn't fall off. It's just sometimes they do.

Dedication:
Days and Days and Days

Some people have dedicated days and days and days to rock climbing. I approached a number of lifelong devotees and asked the single question – How do you feel about rock?

Johnny Dawes:

'I feel grateful to / to rock.

My interest in rock has taken me to a lot of places. And to a lot of shapes. And to a lot of situations. Which have allowed me to / to learn about the world and myself.

And my place in the world.

And to enjoy the happenings that go on around rock: produces soil; produces a wind break; it's a way to get exercise; it's a way to meet other people of like mind; it's a way of expressing one's poetical leanings with the naming of climbs; it's a way of pitting yourself against other people's challenges, which are laid there in aspic for you to try; it's a way of feeling the passage of time when you come back to places you've already known.

And it's everywhere.'

Johnny starred in **Stone Monkey** *(1986) and* **Hard Grit** *(1998), put up epically famous routes like The Quarryman and Indian Face, and moves beautifully on rock.*

Mina Leslie-Wujastyk:

'Gosh, it's so hard to put into words, isn't it?

One of the first words, descriptive words that comes into my mind is freedom. And / So there's this sense of feeling free, I think.

On the rock.

You know, whether that's free physically, or free mentally. Just a certain amount of, like, independence and autonomy and / Yeah! Freedom that you get on the rock / When you feel / when the challenge is in the right place, right, and you feel kind of comfortable, in the zone, and / Yeah.

There's a / and / but there's also this kind of / I like / like this kind of connection. The texture. The feeling between your hand and the rock. And / that kind of / that connection is really nice.

And then, when your body feels strong and fit, there's this connection between / You're holding the rock. But everything's working. Right from your fingertips, up your arms, to your core. You know. All your muscles are kind of working together to create this, kind of, fluid movement, and then your brain is also working to kind

of problem-solve your way through the moves. So /
Yeah!

It's kind of a complex question, isn't it. Because there's a
lot going on when you're / When you're on the rock.

But there's definitely, like / It's like a way of stepping
out. Of a normal existence. I feel like you step into this
almost other-worldly place, mentally and physically for
a while.'

*Mina is a polymath – sponsored climber, yoga teacher,
nutritionist and writer. She co-hosts a podcast with
Hazel Findlay, called* The Curious Climber.

Jesse Dufton:

'I guess the literal interpretation! Because, obviously,
that's the primary sense that I'm interacting with the
rock in. And also, I think it's just something that's just
quite a big part of me. You know, it's something that I've
always done. And it's something that I've committed
a lot of time to. Something that I get a lot of pleasure
from. And a few scars as well.

I don't really think too much about it, because it's so
innate with me, I guess.

I think the thing that I always really enjoy about
climbing is the feeling you get from when you take on
something that's at your limit, but you manage to do
it well. You didn't have a gibbering epic on it. And you

didn't, you know, let your head interfere too much. You just went for it. I think when you / when you do that, the satisfaction you get is what I most enjoy. You'll have done some, like, cool moves that were hard for you and you'll have, kind of, you'll have addressed all the different challenges that the climbing presents to you simultaneously. The physical, the skill, the mental – all at the same time.

But, yeah, I guess it's kind of like a sense of inner calm. A sense of physical exertion. And, for me, I guess, like, kind of a memory of the movement and the / kind of the feelings of the holds. And the feeling of the, like, wind buffeting you. And stuff like that.

But, obviously, it's quite different for me. Because loads of / loads of climbers, you know / You get to go to these amazing places and see the view. And I can't see that. So – it's kind of / My experience is quite different. In some ways. And exactly the same in others.'

Jesse is blind, has been climbing since he was two years old, and is part of the GB paraclimbing team. He featured in Climbing Blind, *leading The Old Man Of Hoy.*

Trevor Massiah:

'I mean, it provides everything, doesn't it? For me.

It provides my livelihood. It provides my greatest pleasures. It provides companionship.

Because it's a very selfish act, climbing, isn't it? But also, it's incredibly social. So, although you're having an experience on your own – the fact that so many people enjoy that same experience means that you have always got someone to share that with. Even though when you're actually climbing it's a very individual thing. So it / [*sigh*] / it just provides so many different things.

So I guess, really, it's a very generous mineral isn't it.

You can depend on it. It's there. What it gives you when you go and immerse yourself in it! Just go rock climbing. And you're guaranteed to have a rewarding experience.

And that could be just hanging out with mates on a sunny day. By the sea and / and doing a bit of scrambling around on rocks. And it's quite relaxed. Or it could be quite intense because, you know, you throw yourself at something that you've been thinking about for a long time / that you know's going to be a challenge. And then you / you know that you've got no guarantee you'll be able to do it. So /

It's a weird relationship, isn't it. I mean – It is a weird / it's a weird thing. Climbing up and coming down. Climbing up, coming down.

Of course – sometimes it's unpleasant. Sometimes it's a bit scary. [*sigh*] / Yeah. I dunno. It's / Yeah.

Sometimes you can complain. You look to your skin and it's ripped to pieces. And then the next day, you're going back for more. It causes you pain, but you just keep coming back. For more.

It's / it's / Yeah. We don't really think about it too much, do we? You know, the actual process of ramming your fingers into these horrible, sharp pockets and cracks and / To a non-climber, it must just be insane. If you could actually, somehow, by virtual reality kind of engage with how it feels – if you had like a VR headset on, and you were actually feeling the pain of / feeling the experience someone was having / but you weren't actually climbing it yourself – you'd be like, *Why the hell would anyone do that?*

I've realised recently how much I like that process of / of creating a climb. Like just / Yeah. Creating a sport route. You watch people climb these routes and everyone's having a / Fairly good climbers will have a very similar experience. Just doing the moves in a certain way. And then – you can see the reaction in people. The rock is there. And it's inanimate. But the emotional response that a climber has, to doing that set of moves, is gonna be / for a genuine climber is gonna be the same.

And it doesn't necessarily have to be difficult. It's just that the joy in moving and exploring the rock to find the holds and work out how to use the holds, in order to stay in balance to move up. It's just a beautiful /

It's like dancing, of course.

It's / it's just / I find it amazing.

It just never seems to get boring.

And there's just no end to it. There's rock everywhere.'

Trevor has been rock climbing and instructing for over thirty-five years. He specialises in coaching and co-owns Rock & Sun (climbing holidays and courses).

Lynn Robinson:

'There's absolutely no right or wrong way up a mountain. You're just meandering, you find your own way up by just your own instinctive feel. For / for the rock. You know – people are different – heights, have different strengths, and different body shapes. It doesn't matter. You / you climb it, and you touch it in different ways.

And just not the / not the touching with your / your hands, but with your feet!

And it's about trust. It's about trust between yourself and the rock. It's absolutely phenomenal. Especially, you know, slabs! Just where you can put your feet, and you just think *Okay, rock – don't spit me off this!* You know. *I want to keep in contact with you here!* And just that trust and that faith, that the, you know / Sometimes the rock will let you and sometimes it won't let you! And you'll / you'll come off. But you absolutely need to have that / that trust. And that understanding of the rock.

I love, say, going to sea cliffs. Down to Cornwall. And that has got a different feel, has the rock. So even / even in Great Britain you can / The rock feels so differently. Like / I mean, sea cliff climbing is just the best! Just the absolute best! Whether it's Gogarth or / or / or whether it's down in Cornwall. Because it has got that saltiness to it. Compared to maybe the outcrops on the outskirts of Manchester and Sheffield that have had that / have got that very industrial feel to them. To the very remote mountains that just feel completely untouched.

So, you know, I just love all the challenges that rock throws at you. And all the different challenges that you / have to use, like I say, whether it's / Yeah! Whether you've been climbing on sea cliffs / When you get home and you've got to wash all your gear in the bath, because they're all just covered in / in / in salt.

Yeah! So it's / It's a beautiful relationship. That's just really enhanced my life. It's not just about the / the physical challenge. It's always so about the mental challenge. When you think about rock, with just / and how you're going to ascend it or traverse it or / there's so many different methods, you know, to / [*sigh*] /

Sometimes I absolutely – hate it! You know. Say for example when you're trying to climb a crack, and you have to fist jam / put / put your fist / fist in to act as a hold. And you just think *Oh my goodness me! My hand! How can I get this in?* You have to just move it. Just by a millimetre – and suddenly – yes! – you've connected. With the rock. And you can use it as a handhold.

But sometimes it takes a lot of time, especially, you know, with smaller hands, and in the summer when everything feels very greasy and hot.

One of the best things I love about rock is that feeling that to get to the top of a mountain or get to the top of a route – you can't do it by walking. It's very special. I think in / Certainly in Britain we have very strong ethics and values which are so, so important in terms of how we climb. Especially what's called traditional climbing, trad climbing, you know, that's just based on / on values. And that, to me / It's not only how I feel about the physical rock but it / The people I've met along the way. You can climb anywhere in the world, and when you say you're a rock climber, it's one big community. And you're instantly understood. You don't have to explain why you're climbing, why you're there to feel the rock. People just know. And it's an instant bond.

And sometimes, you know, when you're on the crag, or on the mountain, and people, like, think they joke / and just saying, 'Why don't you just walk round? Ha ha ha!' and I just think, *You know what? This is my secret. Why I climb. Why I feel the rock. And I'm not going to tell you why I'm not just walking round the path. Because it's my secret. And if you don't climb, and feel the rock, you won't know that.*

And it's very, very special.'

Lynn has devoted her time and attention to rock for over three decades – climbing, working with volunteers and on

guidebooks. She is the BMC President.

Niall Grimes:

'So I was doing a / I'm doing a book called *Boulder Britain*, and I travel round / You get downloads of PDFs of random bouldering areas and you sort of / it's codified words and grid references and stuff like that. And then I go off and find them. You walk off into these places and you don't / you couldn't / you can't always tell what it's going to be like from the descriptions they give. But then you get there, and you behold this piece of rock and it's just so beautiful / it's so /

I was up in Northumberland and I saw about six or seven, eight, nine pieces of rock that were just as beautiful as anything I'd ever seen before.

And / well / it's / you / Your feel for rock is kind of one where you touch and how the / how the texture and temperature of the rock interacts with you.

But it's also the emotional feel. Because, as a climber / It overrides lots of other emotional interactions with it. So when you see it, you understand what the movement is / because that's / that's the amazing thing about rock climbing is the movement, isn't it? That's the thing you don't see until you've been doing it a few years. That's why people who've been doing it for a long time, understand this more than people who've only just started. It's the move, to me, is the beautiful thing. And what it puts your body and mind through.

It's / it's / it's a special thing.

And that's the move. And – again – when you're showing somebody climbing, what they see is the hold. But the move is the understanding of what goes on between all these things, when it's interacting with you. And you see a piece of rock – a lot of arêtes, these things are mostly arêtes – and you can just feel what it's like to be on that piece of rock. And I guess in some ways you're purely on the rock's surface and / which is kind of interesting as it goes so emotionally deep with yourself. In one way you're only on the rock's surface, but I guess you're feeling the mass of the rock underneath it all.

It's the way your hands feel the rock. And the way the / through the / through the rubber on your feet, your foot feels the rock. It's also how your emotions feel / cos it's / that's / that's what keeps me going rock climbing. What my emotions feel when I'm doing a move. And then / and these moves, they just sort of / they make your muscles tingle, when you think about locking an undercut down to your waist, or how / how your / how your forearm feels when it's on a pumped crimp. And these are all how you feel about it. How your body feels about it. And that's for me, what keeps me going on rock climbing. That nourishment.

Which took me a long time to understand. To understand what the move was. But now / now that I understand the move – I can feel the move. And when you see these bits of rock up in Northumberland! I wasn't climbing them, I was looking at them. And you look. My body / Is it like pornography? Where you can / I don't know – is this the right thing? Pornography. Where you can sort of / Imagining sex with the person you look at / and that's /

That's probably a really bad analogy because it's nothing like that at all.

When you see the piece of rock, your muscles, bones and tendons feed off even looking at it.

They feed off it.

If it's the right piece of rock, where you can see the moves, and you can understand what the moves would be on it / You know, your body doesn't even need to climb it. To sustain itself. From this interaction, this emotional interaction. With the piece of rock.

So I really feel rock.

And I / When I see rock, my body feels it. When I touch rock, my body feels it. When I remember rock, my body feels it. '

Niall (Grimer) is another dedicated climber. He has published many books, and hosts an ongoing podcast called **Jam Crack Climbing.**

Geekery:

Paraphernalia

Shark

Rock boots the teeth of the shark
Pointy-precise
Killing it

The way they grip
Backward-pointing
So aggressive

Make fingers
Seem soft as gills or the points
Of dorsal fins

My cupboard a frenzy
Of pointlessly retained worn out
Rock shoes. Fallen teeth

Renewed when their pointed
Tips blunted
And freed the fish

Kit

Each piece of gear is a team-member
A cowgirl's horse
The shepherd's dog

I recall, starting out
The ropes looking feral, skinny, untrained
But now they sit to heel

Metalware trit-trots alongside
Clattering in herds
Of quickdraws and hexes

Chalk bags the pets
Cute fluffy cats or guinea pigs
Snuggling in

I know the history of every friend and wire
Bought here, found there
Given as a gift

The kit that kept me alive, evidenced
By the buckle on that cam, a gouge in that nut
A heritage built up

When he first took me to the Roaches
Gave me twin ropes to feed
And told me not to let go

Neither of us foresaw
How I'd love those ropes
Or how long, and how hard, I would grip

Racking

Betty chooses friends on the left
Nuts on the right
Colour-coded and ranged
From tinies to giant

Chris keeps quickdraws upfront
Rocks and cams to the rear
Smalls and bigs on one hip, mediums on the other
They're an underclipper

Roger overclips. Always
Fully-stocked, hexes to RPs
Whatever the grade or length of pitch
Haunted by that time he lacked a crucial Rock 3

For Luke, half a dozen draws, an even number
For luck. Single set of wires, one to eight
No camming devices
He travels light

Jennifer twiddles her slings and
Snaps them to krabs at the back of her harness
That way, they don't jumble in her gear
Or slide off her shoulders

Dave wraps four-footers athwart his chest
Linked with a screwgate
Short slings cross-slung
No tangling or muddling

Laura racks two clips, one to thirteen
Keeps a set either side. Hunky-dory!
She's done this since her partner
Dropped the large wires in the sea

Divine Law

Like most novices starting out
Had no possessions
Beyond boots, harness, chalk bag, helmet

Tied in
Borrowed one item from the leader
He called it a furkler

Spanish Inquisition of a tool
To prod cams, poke cracks
Fiddle with wires, bash at hexes

Divine law
Decreeing a point of pride
Never to leave a piece of gear behind

The agony! Cuticles bleeding, knuckles scuffed
Wounds at the centre of my palm
Climbing stigmata

Head bowed over each nut
Seconding to see
If I had what it took to devote myself utterly

One piece of kit
Against a whole rack
Made a vow to buy my own nut key

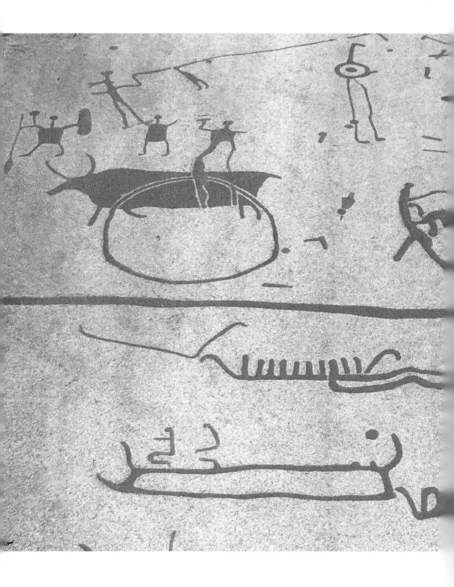

Wonder:
Science or Magic?

Close-hauled

Out sailing, a yacht cannot go nose-on into the wind. It is not possible: akin to trying to climb when you can't reach the starting holds; no progress can be made. But what if you lean out sideways a little – is that a line of crimps? Could you balance on that tiny ledge?

And so we come to my favourite point of sailing. 'Point of sailing' being a technical term referring to the direction of the boat in relation to the wind. Rather than 'What's the point, I'd rather be soloing that VDiff'. But anyway.

As I was saying, my favourite point of sailing is being close-hauled, which is typically around fifty-five degrees off the full force of the blow. When you get this just right, something special happens – for the wind is full in your face but you are still going forwards. It is magic! It shouldn't be happening. Like the bus in Harry Potter where it sucks itself in and slides between traffic, emerging at full speed, everyone unhurt, unbelievably.

Also, when the sails are set just right, you do not fight the helm. Instead, the boat takes on a hunting instinct, slicing into the water, sniffing into the breeze, the edges of the sails trilling with life, with the chase, with the impossibility, with the tension, the core strength, with the pace. It reminds me of taking on a route at the top of your grade but you are fit, focused. It's not hard. You've had a much harder time on a thousand HVSs.

There is a science, of course: to achieve this on a sloop rig both sails are winched in to the max, the mainsail taut and the genoa pegged out, a flayed skin, drum-tight. The gap between them acts as an aerofoil, the same anti-logic that keeps huge metal aeroplanes in the air on their tiny wings.

In order to accommodate this anti-logic, this reality shift, other paradigms bend. In particular, the earth, which we generally experience as horizontal and static, tips. The boat heels over at a wild angle. A flagged foot counterbalancing a barn door suspends you in balletic arabesque.

Close-hauled is also called 'beating'. The fact that beating is my favourite point of sailing should not be lost on fellow climbers. Since when have we taken the easy path? While others spend a Sunday afternoon reading the papers and having a barbecue, what are we doing? When others take the steps with the handrail to get to the top of the chasm, how do we get there? That's right. By the hardest, silliest, most nonsensical and slowest way, moving up the sheer rock.

The Trip

Last June, through absurd serendipity and good fortune, I ended up on a yacht sailing along the Swedish west coast of Bohuslän, anchoring up at various spots and going climbing on the local granite crags. There were five of us – Andy and Siân (who own the boat); an old school friend of Andy's also, unhelpfully, called Andy; and Kathryn who I thought might be a student as she looked very young but turned out to have worked for the civil service for over a decade and was just about to take a posting in Afghanistan. Which all frankly goes to show how old I am.

I had been a little anxious about going on a yacht. A certain prejudice against wealth. A judgment against the boating community, posh knobs who would ask me difficult questions like 'What do you do?' and look down on my £8.99 H&M deck shoes. But it was okay. I'd underplayed the other element in the mix – these people were climbers. And climbers are my people. Climbers are irreverent and make-do and take the piss out of each other while holding ropes and keeping their mates alive. The banter started up almost immediately and I knew it was going to be alright.

It was immensely pleasing to engage in the landscape through saltwater as well as rock. To arrive on the water, walk to the crag and climb, then leave by water. Bohuslän is a shattered coast of thousands of islands; a great place to sail. The interaction of granite and sea was so elemental – unbroken by human-made diesel and car-speed and noise

– it gave the whole week a dream-like quality.

DNA

This tale will illustrate one day, one route. The sun is shining, we are breakfasted and happy and sailing to our next crag in a moderate easterly breeze.

Turning in from open waters, we pinched our way down a long narrow inlet fashioned, like everything else sticking out of the sea, of pink granite. Mainly it looked uninhabited. There were very occasional houses, places to moor up, buoys indicating fish farms and lobster pots. After a while we came to a little floating concrete quay. Lining the side of the yacht with fenders, we came alongside; a couple of us jumped ashore, looped ropes through metal staples and threw the ends back to be hitched on deck.

The moment when the boat is fixed, stable, and the engine – which we used for anchoring/mooring up – can be cut, reminded me of being safe on a climb. That switch from peak of alertness to being out of danger – no one fell in the water, no one's hurt, nothing's damaged – induced the same fugacious brainlessness that can touch me at the top of a route. How after a struggle, I need a second or two to compose myself. Similarly we moored up, and disguised this strange transition by faffing with rucksacks. Two teams, Andy and me, Kathryn and Andy II, four ropes, trad gear with plenty of quickdraws, plenty of cams. A thermos of coffee. Cinnamon pastries. All set, we headed off, walking, from the quay.

A hundred yards up the road there is a footpath off to the right. Not marked on the map, it seemed to lead in the right direction. 'Footpath!' I suggested. This was rejected by the team, quite rightly, as it could have taken us anywhere and we were on a mission – but for your information it does indeed take a scenic way through woods and pop you out at the crag. Nevertheless the walk along the deserted car-free road is also lovely and has better views. We passed an open green where the wilted flower-wreathed rings of the midsummer celebrations dangled from a maypole. A further half-mile on, we arrived at Galgeberget.

The routes are one to two pitches high. Galgeberget rock is quite featured and varied and doesn't have the clean splitter cracks of some of the other local crags. However, there are a couple of especially good mid-grade routes which take obvious bottom-to-top lines.

Swedish grading is, broadly, like French grading but nails. In the same way that Swedish krona have an exchange rate of about ten to the pound but *an expensive ten* (as I write the rate is 1:10.63). So, as someone who might on a good day tackle a friendly F6b+ I found a bunch of the 5s desperate and 6- was my best lead. DNA was 6-. I chose it because Kendrick Lamar had a new album out called *DAMN.* and *DNA* was the second track. Also because we chatted to some locals who recommended DNA and its neighbour Palimpsest (5+) as the routes of the crag.

DNA did that granite thing of rewarding shapes, making me throw moves. It invited a range of techniques – jamming, laybacking, pinches and crimps. It allowed me to rest my arms on the deal that I sacrificed one other area of my body (twisted feet, torqued core) to pure pain. A continuous crack over three tiers of rock, DNA had a compulsive quality, the pull of great gear and a great line, the improbable victory of faith over strength, of desire over what's sensible, moments of teetering on shiny crystal footholds, of believing in flared jams. I moved up, on the cusp of staying on and falling off; that close-hauled angle of improbability.

Thirty-five metres later I was making a belay. I had one of those 'I was made to live my life like this' flushes of happiness. Andy followed. From height, I watched Siân approaching along the mystery footpath (she had braved the exploration, and led us home that way) wearing her wide straw hat. I couldn't see the boat or the water. It seemed fantastical that we were here at all.

Heeling

This metaphor of beating, of sailing close-hauled – remember I mentioned how some basic paradigms have to tilt in order to make it work? In order to facilitate sliding through the impossible like the Harry Potter bus?

For me, to make living on the edge work, as a lifestyle, certain accepted norms had to be turned upside-down a little. So my career fell on its side, my relationships have not provided a steady deck, my social status is unstable, kinky, tipped. Is this the price to pay for sailing into the wind?

I doubt there is a golden incontrovertible rule. Everyone is individual and almost anything is possible. But is there a link between freedom of thought, freedom of movement and some other things being a little different? You may be going on all sorts of trips, but if the framework of the rest of your life is conservative, how far are you really travelling? How far do you have to heel over to sail at fifty-five degrees? And is that science – or magic?

I know my life dips in and out of that perfect angle. Sometimes I take it easy for a bit, cruising along on a beam reach, enjoying the comfort of habit and the pleasures of relaxing. And then another time I will have bitten off more than I can chew, tried too hard, steered into the breeze and put my sails flogging.

But I know when I'm happiest. And I'd like to say it's with the wind behind me, goose-winged, gin and tonic in hand, chatting amicably on a level deck. But we all know I'd be lying.

Underneath the Arches

Underneath the Arches (E2), Mewsford Arches,
Pembrokeshire, UK

The name encapsulates it: avenues of beech trees with interlinking boughs; Victorian train stations adorned with looping wrought iron; the awe-inspiring ceilings of medieval cathedrals – delicate, towering, lit with beams from stained glass windows. And this is the essence of Underneath the Arches as for pitch after horizontal pitch the cut-away cliff is sculpted into ancient and astonishing vaults, dappled with refracted light.

There was no indication the day would be heavenly. We drove over early on a Saturday morning, mid-winter, unprepossessing, the usual drizzle past Newport, with no plan of what to do, a few single-pitch classics perhaps. Mileage. Then Barbary Lion had an idea, made a call or two to check the tides and in a jiffy we were heading for Underneath the Arches. I'd never heard of it, didn't know what I was getting into, was blissfully unaware of the litany of requirements necessary for this route and the fact they all came together that day was nothing short of a miracle. This is what is needed:

1. A time outside the bird ban. For pretty much half the year the route's out of bounds. In addition, late summer/autumn would find you clawing through mounds of guano;

2. No Ministry of Defence firing in Range East;

3. Low tides in the afternoon;

4. Little or no swell;

5. A dry day, as is usual with climbing. And possibly not after a stretch of heavy rain to minimise seepage through the belly of the world;

6. You've remembered your abseil rope;

7. A full day to dedicate to the venture;

8. A team where both parties lead at least E2; don't mind doing a ten pitch route that's utterly inescapable and appears somewhat unrescuable; are willing to do the furthest walk-in in Pembroke, to Mewsford, midway between the two car parks; are reconciled, despite the not insignificant effort involved, to gain merely two 'E Points' apiece for the entire day as calculated by the harsh grading system promoted by the Ultimate Sanction.

It doesn't sound like much, perhaps. But what with one thing and another maybe once in a blue moon do all these factors come together. We got lucky that day. We were blessed. An early start in January/February I suggest would be the time to summon the gods on your bleeding knees and make it happen.

It's a two hundred and forty-metre right-to-left traverse. Cowboy and Cowgirl know every inch of the Range and their pioneering new-routing spirit is exemplified here. For this is the Wild West of rock climbing and every ascent of Underneath the Arches will always be an adventure.

This is why: the route travels the cave systems beneath Mewsford. Picture this: four rope-lengths in and you're at a hanging stance on an exposed arête. It's a calm day but nonetheless, just below, the gnashing waves echo and lick at you. To your left the route disappears into the dark, curving back in an immense semi-circle, a hemisphere chewed out of the foot of the cliff by a hungry sea. The leader a small figure going crab-wise in the preposterous, damp amphitheatre. The modest swell is funnelling into the back of the cave, smashing over the ropes and swashing over where the second must follow, sucking back into the churning moiling ruckus where you will go, yes, if you slip up on the soaking footholds. Only two pieces of gear are visible from here; you visualise leap-frogging a friend along the break, a trick of security, tip-toeing the wet rim before timing a panic-stricken sprint between sets of white water in the din of the greedy roar. On top of all this, oppressively looming above your helmet, is the most gob-smacking roof ever, an unbelievable roof, it stretches from the back of the cave perfectly horizontally out to the far sky, for what? Ten metres? Fifteen? More? Which means that above your head balance innumerable tons of limestone. Right over your head. Such a weight of it. Should it go, your body would never be found.

Here you are then. Committed. Pitch after pitch in this underworld where escape is impossible and rescue seems, at best, implausible. From the stance my mind drifts. I try to calculate the mechanics of recovery, in the event of an accident. With roofs like these they wouldn't be able to abseil in. Not anywhere. A boat sent by the coastguard maybe, a soft rib, nudged into the back of the cavern, the heaving zone at the junction of the land and the sea; someone in a wetsuit with a buoyancy aid who'll cradle your damaged body as your shocked partner lowers you into the foam. Is there mobile reception there? I can't remember checking. Most of the Range doesn't seem to have a signal. So I doubt it. The improbability of being extricated distracts me.

And such a beast! The longest route in Pembroke by a country mile. Decent-length pitches: twenty-four metres, thirty metres, thirty-nine metres. I tend to reckon on roughly an hour a pitch which doesn't add up at all for a ten pitch route where sundown's at 4.30pm. We alternated leads with the second carrying half a litre of water and a small wrapper of biscuits. It's such a trip; the further you climb in, the more compelled you are. There is no halfway exit gully. Vista after vista after vista appears but it's impossible to say how far it goes on and where the end is; only that you have to crack on because no one's coming down here to get you. I recall a certain gracelessness on the crux, an English 5c belly-flopping shuffle. I was grateful that no one could see me! But it was mainly important to get on with it quickly and do it clean.

But it's beautiful. Oh. I forgot! There's one other essential criterion. Choose a day with sun. As if there aren't enough requirements already. But really: choose sun. In mid-January, the sun confines itself to a low arc over the sea; loiters at the door like a friend who's popped by but can't sit down because they're actually meant to be somewhere else; it hugs the winter horizon and thereby bowls its cool, bright, magnificent light right into the very back of every undercut cavern for the whole route; it is your companion all day long. Without sun Underneath the Arches could be somewhat like traversing a partly-flooded road-tunnel hectic with passing HGVs. With sun it is a sparkling world, touched by the glittering hem of the sea-god's gown, lit with glints from the golden spokes of the sun-god's chariot.

On topping out at the walk-off gully, Cowgirl and Cowboy were waiting there, squatting on their heels, angels carved in toppling stone, smiling. It turned out the Lion had sent them a quick text in the morning. And there they were, hours later, keeping vigil in the gloaming of the upper world where the grass grows and the ground is flat, the pub is a simple walk away and prayer doesn't come quite as naturally.

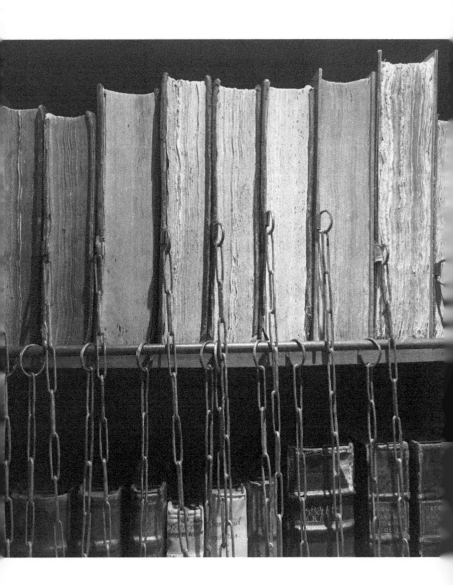

Edification:
The Smile

The Smile (E1), Lower Sharpnose, Cornwall, UK

Lower Sharpnose always reminds me of books. Three of them, teetering on their spines, propped up in the shale and mud of the Culm coast. How come they are still here, paper-thin, when the Atlantic batters them twice a day? The rock a compact grey interlaced with quartzite veins; white writing on a dark page. The Smile is the easiest route of any on the main faces. Traces a row of crystal letters diagonally across the south side of the North Fin before striking directly up the steepening headwall. In a flurry of exhaustion you flop over the top which turns out to be a disembodied strip of rock, tattered and dog-eared, the up-ended pages of a novel that got damp then dried, over and over again. You belay with your face to the setting sun and the tide coming in. It's a thrilling route in one of the most unbelievable settings in the world. Go climb it before it falls down! The End.

Commonality:
Curriculum Vitae

For years, under Hobbies and Pastimes, my C.V. said 'Rock Climbing – a particular love of sea cliffs'. I've realised this is not the information that is generally required. I should have put my typical – or, actually, highest – grade, how long I've been climbing, the most impressive location names.

But when I meet people, I'm interested in what they love.

Understanding:
What Language Do We Speak?

There are many tongues. The language of food, for example. Recently I negotiated bramble-cutting with the neighbours through the lingua franca of chocolate chip cookies. Football is a classic common tongue – as exemplified by the legendary WWI match across the trenches. Though that, of course, began with the language of song. Music is a code across time and place and species. We respond emotionally to birdsong, whale song, Bach's *Sonata No.5 in F minor* from three centuries ago.

What about the language of rock climbing? We understand each other when we talk about crimps and gastons and jams. We know what we mean by exposed and chossy and bold. I find delight in its encyclopaedic precision, onomatopoeic punchiness and occasional comic restraint. I use climbing analogies, constantly. An administrative ordeal, *like a ten pitch route, leading every pitch*. A delicate conversation, *tip-toeing up a slab*. Climbing language is one important way I process and comprehend the world.

However, it is not universal. It is cliquey, exclusive, a secret terminology. Climb-speak, for the uninitiated, can be thoroughly alienating. Which means I sometimes switch to other vernaculars, other metaphors, other sports – like sailing or snooker – to communicate an issue or a feeling or a technique.

Maybe it is best spoken with hands.

Comfort:

The Chronicles

Hands

My hands a landscape eroded
By the forces of granite and plastic

Tips smooth as tumbled pebbles
Swollen joints a chain of lakes leading

To a delta of calluses where fingers
Run into the hand-mass. Classical

Indoor-jug-formation of skin rucked up
On each pinky at the middle phalanx

The open palm a savanna where
Quartzite and gneiss trample and graze

On the backs, cuticles ragged
From nibbling by limestone mice

Knuckles grubbed-up and gouged
By wild boar grit. Blue vein

Rivers, distended from recurring
Flash-floods of de-pumping

Flow over the dorsal plains
Where, gradually, crevasses and hillocks

Crack and crumple up, a legacy
Of exposure, time and over-use of chalk

Sun-damaged liver spots
Settle and spread, a moraine of choss

Panoramic hands – weathered and worn
Becoming more like the rocks

Guides

My first set of guidebooks
For Avon, Cornwall, Wye Valley, Dorset
A mismatched hotchpotch
Of second-hand cast-offs and gifts
From every birthday and Christmas

The second lot of guides purchased myself
For Avon, Cornwall, Wye Valley, Dorset
Felt like an accomplishment
I'd lasted the course! Matured, grown
Plus the latest style had updated topos

When it came to the third round
Of Avon, Cornwall, Wye Valley, Dorset
I looked at my shelf and thought
Has the rock really changed all that much?
But I like to invest, show my support

The fourth batch of guides
For Avon, Cornwall, Wye Valley, Dorset
Came from the Internet, downloads
Like everyone else, I'm squinting and checking
My phone on the belays, pitch by pitch

The latest print copies are super-sized
For Avon, Cornwall, Wye Valley, Dorset
Full colour photos, coffee table books
I goon at the hard lines I did once, circle
A new tick-list of all the easy routes

Ruth's Rules

Onto my third A5 Single Cash hardback recording
Every route I've ever climbed, since the beginning
In 1998. One route per line. Rigorous criteria for E-Points
Set out in Book One: 'On lead, no falls. 10 pitch E2
Still counts as 2 E-points. Ruth's Rules.' With an arrow
To that year's tally – eight

Date, route name and crag, climbing partner, grade
Specifics of style – square brackets for seconding
Scored through with a dotted line if not clean, solid line for a fail
Uber-nerdy. Repeats of 3-bolt wonders at the local quarry
Written down over and over again
No route too small or too great. The occasional note –

'Backed off from rib – no gear!' – 'Led pitches 5 & 7'
'Ace route, amazing territory!' – 'Rested taking out friend
Needed two hands' – 'First two bolts clipped, all quickdraws in'
'Really really really 3*' – 'Jamming on crozzles. Mmmm'
'Green and loose!' – 'Hard and polished!' – 'Got knee stuck!'
'DOGGED' – 'Darn tufas' – 'OH MY GOD!! Bonkers'

All the toil and fear and blood and injuries and fun condensed
Into four lines at the end of each year – Number of Routes;
Hardest Trad; Hardest Sport; E-Points – an almanac
Over two thousand ascents. Accountancy of life on the rocks
In credit. A comfort. Risks taken prudently
Kept out of the red and survived in the black

JOY

Joy:
Rocking the Lexicon

Bedrock is a place of ultimate stability, something you can trust. It will not move or shift or slyly shirk its responsibilities. Bedrock remains. You can lie down on bedrock and it will still be there in the morning.

Solid as a rock (see *Bedrock*, above).

The phrase *She is a rock* means that she is utterly reliable and strong at heart and also a good soul.

To *rock* is a rhythmic, soothing oscillation; up and down like a lucky-cat's paw, or side to side as a metronome keeping time. It is the tempo of lullabies, how babies are calmed to sleep. My mother could spot me in school assemblies, apparently, as I was the only child rocking.

Rock bottom is the worst possible situation, emotionally, financially or spiritually.

Finding yourself *between a rock and a hard place* is being trapped between two appalling options, with no easy, cost-free solution.

You rock! means you're really entertaining and great to hang out with.

Rock the boat is to disrupt the status quo. There is a confidence to it. Making little waves splash over the sides, and watching them.

Rock my world means disruption of the deep core. Often with positive connotations as if, by being comprehensively shaken up, all your atoms and fibres and feelings become energised. It is the experience of aliveness, of song, of transformative joy.

Acknowledgments

Climbing Partners

Thank you to my ongoing climbing partners, especially Emma Alsford, Natalie Barwood, Alan/Ginger Britton, Jess Carr, Henry Castle, Andy Collins, Mandi Dodson, Sandro Gromen-Hayes, Martin Kocsis, McKenzie Lloyd-Smith, Trevor Massiah, Robyn Nelson and Lynne Williams.

Writing

Thank you to many of the above, and also Floyd Ballantyne, Ron Barraclough, Joachim Berntsson, Tony Dunlop, Pat and Tony Hill, Pedro Muñoz, Ian Parnell, Dave Talbot; Natalie Berry and Alan James at UKC; my technical reviewers Trevor Massiah and Ruth Taylor; Romany Fig for proof-reading; Dan and Helen Kent and William Lambie at Powerful Ideas Press.

Contributors

Thank you to Clara, Ebony, Alice, Johnny Dawes, Mina Leslie-Wujastyk, Jesse Dufton, Trevor Massiah, Lynn Robinson, Niall Grimes and Hazel Findlay for contributing content.

Thank you to the following photographers and artists:

> Back cover – Stephen Reid
> Desert tower (page 14) – Dan Donovan
> Author portrait (page 129) – McKenzie Lloyd-Smith
> Still from *The Salty Dance Floor* (page 150) – Sandro Gromen-Hayes

Herring gull sketch (page 158) – Romany Fig

Nut-slot (page 168) – Special mention to Ellis and Eddie from Dorset

All other images, artworks and cartoons by the author.

Publishers

Thank you to editors of the publications in which these articles and cartoons first appeared:

'Bewilderment: Past the Peak', *Climb* magazine (Greenshires Group Ltd), Issue 87, May 2012

'Hurt: Aren't You the Climber?' first published as 'Identity Theft', *Summit* magazine, Issue 67, Autumn 2012

'Awe: Underneath the Arches', *Climb* magazine (Greenshires Group Ltd), Issue 98, April 2013

'Edification: The Smile' – first published as number 86 of 'The Best 100 Climbs in Britain', *Climb* magazine (Greenshires Group Ltd), Issue 100, June 2013

'Outrage: The Wall II' first published as 'The Wall by Counter-Monkey', *Climb* magazine (Greenshires Group Ltd), Issue 109, March 2014

'Confusion: Better than Sex?', *Climb* magazine (Greenshires Group Ltd), Issue 112, June 2014

'Companionship: Pick and Mix', *Summit* magazine, Issue 74, Summer 2014

'Thankfulness: Art of the Rest' first published as 'The Subtle Art of Anti-Ambition', *Climb* magazine (Greenshires Group Ltd), Issue 115, September 2014

'Love: Rock Is the Earth's Truth', *Climb* magazine

(Greenshires Group Ltd), Issue 118, December 2014

'Pride: Climb Like a Girl', *Climb* magazine (Greenshires Group Ltd), Issue 124, July 2015

'Wonder: Science or Magic?' first published as 'Bohuslän: Science or Magic?', *Climb* magazine (Greenshires Group Ltd), Issue 141, October/November 2017

'Exclusion: The Perfect Line' first published as 'The Perfect Line: Naming and Claiming', *UKClimbing.com*, 19 June 2019

'Dislocation: Cyborg-climbers – Come to Your Senses!', *UKClimbing.com*, 16 January 2020

'Respect: Top Tips for Transitions', *The Professional Mountaineer*, Issue 29, Spring 2020

References

Barad, Karen (2007), *Meeting the Universe Halfway: Quantum Physics and the Entanglement of Matter and Meaning*, Duke University Press, Durham and London.

Berry, Natalie (2018), 'Ascending Afghanistan: Hanifa Yousoufi summits Noshaq', *UKClimbing.com*, available at <(https://www.ukclimbing.com/articles/features/ascending_afghanistan_hanifa_yousoufi_summits_noshaq-11482)>.

Dobner, Sarah-Jane & Gromen-Hayes, Sandro (2018), *The Salty Dance Floor*, available at <https://www.youtube.com/watch?v=mm07hLWBFc8>.

Moffat, Gwen (2018), *Summit* magazine, Issue 92, Winter 2018.

Rossiter, Penelope (2007), 'Rock Climbing: On Humans, Nature and Other Nonhumans', *Space and Culture*, 10(2), 292–305.

Thomas, I. (1967), 'A Question Unanswered', in University of New England Mountaineering Club (Eds.), *The New England Tablelands: A guide to bushwalking, caving, rockclimbing* (pp. 85-87), Armidale, NSW, Australia: University of New England Mountaineering Club.

Ward, Meghan, (2010), 'Ban on Route Names Sparks Debate', *Alpinist*, available at <(http://www.alpinist.com/doc/web10f/newswire-route-names-ban-sweden)>.

Wigglesworth, Jennifer (2019), 'What's in a Name? Sexism in Rock Climbing Route Names', *The Society Pages*, available at <(https://thesocietypages.org/engagingsports/2019/01/07/whats-in-a-name-sexism-in-rock-climbing-route-names/)>.

Glossary

ATC
: A branded belay device. ATC stands for 'Air Traffic Controller'.

Back-and-footing
: A way of tackling chimneys – back against one wall, feet pushing against the other.

Barn door
: Where your body swings away from the crag, as a door on hinges. Usually unhelpful.

Belay
: (i) Noun: the location where you tie in safely at the end of a pitch; also a shortening of 'belay device', the metal plate designed to brake the rope; and

(ii) Verb: the act of managing your partner's ropes while they climb.

Belayer
: The person managing the climber's ropes.

BMC
: British Mountaineering Council.

Bold
: Scary climbing with little protection.

Bolts
: Metal loops ('staples') or hangers permanently glued or screwed into the rock.

Bomber
: Fantastic gear placement. Confidence-boosting.

Bouldering
: Low-level climbing without ropes, often protected by mats.

Bucket
: A giant hold. Also known as a 'jug'.

Bumble
: To potter about happily on climbs with no particular ambition.

Cams	Spring-loaded devices with metal lobes, which grip the surrounding rock. Good for parallel-sided cracks. Also called 'friends'.
Chocks	Chunky hexes or nuts.
Choss(y)	Territory which is loose, broken, rubbishy, dangerous, ugly and messy.
Clean	(i) To climb a route with no falls or support from the rope; and
	(ii) To take the gear and quickdraws out of the rock.
Crank	Pull hard on a hold.
Crimp	A tiny but positive handhold which rewards fingers made of steel. Thumbs can stack on top of fingertips.
Crozzly	Friable, hairy-knobbly rock surface. Painful to climb and disconcerting to protect.
Crush	Succeed with macho panache (usually a hard boulder problem).
Crux	The most difficult move or section on a route.
Disco leg	A phenomenon whereby your leg begins to shake uncontrollably. Commonly caused by stress positions on slabs or pure fear.
Dog	Hanging on the rope, pulling on gear, etc. The antithesis of climbing a route clean.
Dyno	A 'dynamic' move where you leap, foot-free, to a distant handhold.

E1	The lowest Extreme grade. Walls tend to be steep enough that you don't hit anything when you fall. You start to realise how frightening HVSs are.
E2-E10 etc	Harder Extreme climbs. The higher the number the more technically difficult, exposed or dangerous the route.
Eliminate	A route which ignores all the obvious lines.
English[x]	English grade of technical difficulty.
Exposed	Climbing with a big feel – because it's high up, or undercut, say. Exposure makes the experience way more intense.
F[x]	French sport climbing grades. Focused on technical difficulty. The higher the number/letter etc, the harder it is.
Flash	Climbing a route clean, first go, but having benefited from tips, videos, inspection, etc beforehand.
Friends	See 'Cams'.
Gaston	A specialist move designed to make progress on unhelpful, vertical holds in front of you: grip sideways, palm rockwards, thumb down and chicken-wing your elbow.
Gear	All the metalware – quickdraws, nuts, cams, etc. More associated with trad paraphernalia.
GriGri	A branded belay device, with assisted braking, used in sport climbing.
Gripped	Terrified.

Hard Severe	Ah! The sweet spot! My favourite grade – great lines, good gear, but never out of control. At least, that's the aim.
Hexes	Irregular, hexagonal metal chocks which wedge into slots in the rock. Commonly large, hollow and clanking.
HVS	Hard Very Severe – the gatekeeper grade – classically so horrific that climbers are warded off from tackling the Extremes.
Jam	A way of climbing cracks, where you shove your fingers/hands/forearm/feet etc in and torque them so you don't fall out.
Jug	See 'Bucket'.
Karabiner/ Krab	A metal clip. Screwgate karabiners are locking krabs.
Layback	A way of climbing sideways holds: set up opposing forces by pulling with your hands and simultaneously pushing your feet away. Strenuous.
Lead/Leader	The person, in trad or sport, who climbs first and places protection/clips bolts on the way. Potential for large/scary/nasty falls. Known as the 'sharp end'.
Line	(i) A gorgeous, natural feature – like a crack, or a groove, or an arête, etc – which just calls out to be climbed; and
	(ii) Where the route goes.

Mantleshelf	(i) Noun: a baffling flattish ledge, at height, with no useful footholds with which to gain access; and
	(ii) Verb: climbing such an obstacle. Techniques range from the stylish out-of-deep-end-of-swimming-pool-arm-press to classic belly flop.
Multi-pitch	A climb made up of two or more pitches.
Nuts	Lumps of metal on wire. Different sizes from tiny (RPs – which can be 2mm across) to about as big as a clementine. On lead, you slot them into crevices in the rock. Also called 'wires'.
Onsight	Climbing a route, ground-up, without any prior knowledge (save reading the guidebook, which is allowed).
Pitch	A unit of climbing, like a chapter of a book. The leader goes first, belays, brings the second up, and that is one pitch. Pitches are typically ten to fifty metres long.
Polish	Where the rock has been so over-climbed, it has buffed up to a glassy sheen.
Pumped	When your forearms swell up and go solid, like an over-pumped bike tyre, from gripping on too hard for too long.
Quickdraws	Two karabiners joined by a length of tape. One krab clips to the gear/bolt and the other clips to the rope.

Rack	(i) Noun: the gear you take with you to climb a route; and
	(ii) Verb: the act of clipping that equipment onto your harness/sling/body in preparation to lead.
Redpoint	Climbing a route clean, having fallen off on previous attempts. A sport climbing technique
Rockover	A move where you shift your bodyweight from one foot to the other, often diagonally sideways. Typically requiring commitment and balance, rather than strength.
Safe	At the top of a pitch, when the leader has built a belay and clipped themselves in. At this point the leader calls down – 'Safe!' – whereupon the second, who has been belaying, can let go of the ropes.
Second	The person, in trad or sport, who follows the leader and takes out the gear and quickdraws. They have a rope above them, which makes seconding much safer than leading (exceptions for traverses, but we'll ignore that).
Slab	An off-vertical climbing surface, like a very steep roof. Harder on the calves than the arms.
Sling	A loop of high strength fabric.
Smear	A footwork technique whereby you pad up a blank wall and stick it with a combination of friction and faith.
Solo	Climbing at height, without ropes. Serious consequences for a fall.

Sport   Roped climbing where you clip bolts, rather than place gear. At the top, the leader generally lowers to the ground, rather than belaying at height. It is typically quicker, safer and more comfortable than trad. The rock has tempting dot-to-dots of silver bolts.

Spotting   A safety practice to protect the boulderer or leader before they have any gear in. Those on the ground (spotters) get their hands ready for a catch, or to guide the climber to the mat.

Staples   See 'Bolts'.

Stick   Not slip.

Take   Hold the climber's weight on the rope. Also a call when the climber wants this – 'Take!' If it happens mid-route, it means they haven't climbed the line clean.

Thrutch   A three-dimensional, floundering style of ascent, involving all body parts simultaneously. Exhausting and graceless. Quintessentially trad.

Topo   Photos or diagrams of crags in guidebooks/on the web which have the lines of routes marked on them.

Trad   'Traditional' roped climbing where you place protection on lead from gear that you're carrying (usually clipped to your harness), and the second follows, taking all the gear out. The cliffs look untouched.

VDiff   Very Difficult – straight-forward, easy trad climbing, as long as it's not too polished. A good grade for bumbling.

VS   Very Severe – as it sounds. VS climbing can hammer you to the ground, with only minimal glory.

Wires   See 'Nuts'.

XS   A route that's too appallingly loose to receive a real grade. You really should get off now.

Zawn   A steep-sided, narrow inlet on the coast – dark and terrifying and usually filled with battering waves.